WHY HUMILITY MATTERS

WHY HUMILITY MATTERS

The radical idea of the practice of humility

JOHN NORSWORTHY

Why Humility Matters
Published by ConsultEd Publishing
45 Bathurst Crescent, Pyes Pa
Tauranga
New Zealand

© 2021 John Norsworthy

ISBN 978-0-473-56332-5 (Softcover)
ISBN 978-0-473-56334-9 (ePUB)
ISBN 978-0-473-56335-6 (Kindle)

Production & Typesetting:
Andrew Killick
Castle Publishing Services
www.castlepublishing.co.nz

Cover design:
Paul Smith

Unless otherwise stated, scriptures are taken from the HOLY BIBLE, NEW INTERNATIONAL VERSION®. NIV®. Copyright© 1973, 1978, 1984 by International Bible Society. Used by permission of Zondervan. All rights reserved.

Or from the New King James Version®. Copyright © 1982 by Thomas Nelson, Inc. Used by permission. All rights reserved.

ALL RIGHTS RESERVED

No part of this publication may be reproduced,
stored in a retrieval system, or transmitted
in any form or by any means, electronic, mechanical,
photocopying, recording or otherwise,
without prior written permission from the author or publisher.

DEDICATION

In the light of the 'culture wars' and world events in recent years, particularly in the days following the pandemic and political turmoil of 2020, I dedicate this book to all citizens who identify themselves as Christians, and are asking the question, 'How should I now live?' This book addresses an important aspect of what we as believers should do in the contemporary culture.
As Proverbs 14:34 teaches, righteousness, the virtue of people, makes a nation great. Humility is an essential part of this nation-exalting righteousness.

If my people, who are called by my name, will humble themselves and pray and seek my face and turn from their wicked ways, then I will hear from heaven, and I will forgive their sin and heal their land.
(2 Chronicles 7:14)

God opposes the proud, but shows favour to the humble... Humble yourselves before the Lord, and He will lift you up. (James 4:6-10)

Humility matters!

CONTENTS

Preface	9
Introduction	11
1. Defining Humility – And my intended posture in writing	15
2. Humility in the Ancient World – The counter-cultural nature of humility	21
3. Humility in Ancient Israel – Introducing 'the God factor'	25
4. Humility in the Story of Christ – Focusing on humility in the Gospels	35
5. The Practice of Humility – As taught in the Epistles	43
6. The Practice of Humility – From our position in Christ	49
7. The Practice of Humility – In the imitation of Christ	55
8. The Practice of Humility – In marriage	59
9. The Practice of Humility – In contrast to false humility	65
10. The Practice of Humility – In Christian community	73
11. The Practice of Humility – In leadership and the workplace	81
12. The Practice of Humility – In the face of opposition	95
13. The Practice of Humility – In our lives	103
14. The Practice of Humility – In working out God's great plan	113
Appendix 1: Contrasting life in the natural with life in the spiritual	120
Appendix 2: Living in the light of grace – Licence, legalism or liberty?	122
Background Reading	125
Also by John Norsworthy	127

PREFACE

As we all do, I often find myself facing an issue in life that requires wisdom to know what is needed in the circumstance, and the confidence to do it. As a student of the Bible, my disposition is to ask the question, 'What does the Bible say?' I am convinced that the Bible, as the inspired Word of God, has something to say to inform us about every issue in life. If I gain some idea of what it has to say about the issue in hand, I can gain confidence to make good decisions and pursue them with single-mindedness.

Over the years, I have worked with teachers in Christian schools. They have been keen to teach their subject or topic in hand from a biblical perspective. Often they have realised that they really didn't know what the Bible had to say that was relevant to the topic. Biblical literacy applied to all of life was often in short supply. I figured I could do my part in meeting this need.

It was this quest to present a clear understanding of a biblical rationale behind a topic or practice that lead me to write my previous books about things cultural and things scientific. And it is in this vein that I write this short book.

I have confined myself to unpacking Scripture rather than repeating what others have said on the topic. Hence there is no list of references at the end. But inevitably, readers will see some things I write that are much like what they have heard before. As I have said before about my writing, I hope to keep it simple, keep it short, and keep it faithful to the truth.

In this short book I hope to show how the practice of humility is a major theme of the Bible, in particular the New Testament. As I embarked upon explaining the thread of the topic through the Bible, it became clear that the Epistles in the New Testament were where the most teaching about the practice of humility occurred. Consequently, I have selected a particular aspect of humility emphasised by a book (Epistle) to shape the way I have unwrapped the topic. I attempt to show how the Bible teaches that humility is an essential component of the way to exercise good leadership, to live in family and in a church, and to influence people and communities that exhibit divisiveness and social inequities.

I am internally challenged as I write this book. I find myself asking, 'Are you writing this as an exercise in arrogance?' and then reflecting, 'No, I sincerely want people to receive the truth found in God's Word. I want God to be glorified.' But I repeatedly remind myself to keep my ego out of my efforts.

I am grateful to those who have critiqued drafts of this book and encouraged me in the process, and to those who have proofread and assisted in the publishing process. Thank you.

INTRODUCTION

Around AD 165, news came to the city of Rome of a new infectious disease spreading from the east. Infectious diseases were part of life in those days, but this one was different. It came with utterly gruesome symptoms, including fever, chills, nausea, vomiting and diarrhoea. It snuck up on people as the symptoms typically showed up two weeks or so after it had been contracted. Its signature characteristic was the development of horrible black pocks over the body. They formed scabs which left disfiguring scars. It became apparent that these pocks formed inside the alimentary track too. Diarrhoea turned from red to black as the disease lingered in the body. Often victims would cough up or excrete scabs. Suffering would continue for two or three weeks before the illness finally subsided or killed them. It was apparent that Rome was experiencing smallpox.

The plague came in waves for a generation, and killed possibly as many as 10 percent of the people of the Roman Empire. The armies were decimated and wars were called off. It swept through all strata of society. In the year AD 189, it was reported that about 2,000 people died per day in the crowded city of Rome.

Most of all, the disease spread fear. People implored the

gods to save them. The masses of people who were not aristocrats received no help to ease their suffering. Thousands were left abandoned on the streets and in the fields to suffer and die. No-one wanted to go near them. Even their own families, if there were any of them left, abandoned them. Apparently, the gods had seen fit to torture them to death.

And yet in the middle of all this horror, there were a few people out in the streets, caring for the sick, feeding them, washing them and when necessary burying them. Somebody cared! In the mid 3rd century, when the plague hit again, these people cared again. These people were risking their own lives to care for those struck down with the plague. They carried the rejection of others because they cared for 'the living dead'. Who were these people?

These risk-takers were known to meet in their houses. They were apparently not religious in the overt sense. They were not into routines of rituals and rules to please the gods. Some called them atheists – meaning 'without gods'. They were despised by many, especially the aristocrats, because they would not bow to them or to Caesar. They were not weak-willed, as they were prepared to take a course of action that would incur the wrath of the State. In an age when education was only for the elite, they educated their own children to think differently. They cared for the sick and vulnerable. It appeared that they lived according to a radically different worldview. Their ideas about what was real, about what was right and wrong, about what was valuable, about caring for others were strangely different!

Why was their attitude and practice so different? This

book attempts to unpack the source of and the teaching about humility that underpinned the thinking of these people who were called Christians.

1

DEFINING HUMILITY
AND MY INTENDED POSTURE IN WRITING

We are watching the wrap-up of a major sporting event on television. The most valuable player is announced and interviewed. In response to questions, they point out that they were not necessarily outstanding by themselves but, because the team around them played so well, they were able to do what they did well. Most of us respond positively to this kind of expression of humility, and would be pleased to see that they are 'grounded'.

In most Western countries, or at least in New Zealand where I live, there are many for whom this kind of humility is regarded as an attitude to be admired. But this value of humility is not universal. There are many places in the world where pride and even arrogance are admired. And in places where humility is admired, there are many who overtly don't aspire to humility. Some of those we see in the public sphere cause us, who believe in the value of humility, to cringe. And then there is an element of pride in us all – yes, even when we admire humility, we are all inclined to be proud even of our own humility!

The words humble, humbled and humility are used for a variety of attitudes, circumstances and actions. The common idea is of a person seeing themselves as being low or being put low. Lowliness can be passive or active. It can be an intrapersonal attitude or idea, or an interpersonal act of lowliness. I find the table below a useful way to clarify the various uses of the word *humility*.

	(Intra)personal	Interpersonal
Passive	(1) Low self-esteem, feeling of shame	(2) Humiliation, imposed, inflicted shame
Active (deliberate choice)	(3) Self-abasement (often attempting to overcome a low self-esteem)	(4) Practised humility (often stemming from an accurate self-esteem)

Virtuous humility is not depression or a poor self-esteem, and with a feeling of shame, (1) in the chart. Such feelings of worthlessness usually lead to passive weakness and despair, unless there is an offer of hope in sight.

Virtuous humility is not humiliation, (2) in the chart. Humiliation is being put down by others. It may be a deliberate choice of others, a form of what we call bullying these days. It may be thrust upon the person by the attitude of the whole of the society in which you live. Being born an outcast is an example of this form of humiliation. Humiliation is often internalised as shame or low self-esteem. In contrast, humility, as focused on in this book, is an active choice to put oneself low in relation to others, often into a position of potential humiliation.

Nor is it a putting down of oneself, sincerely or hypocritically, (3) in the chart. Self-abasement to achieve a sense of satisfaction or righteousness can lead to a reinforcement of low self-esteem or it can lead to a sense of self-righteousness, a self-centred pride. This is sometimes called false humility. The humility we are focusing on in this book is not showy. It is not this false humility.

In this book the focus is on the active interpersonal practice of humility, (4) in the chart. This form of humility is based on a realistic understanding of self and others. It is the opposite of pretension. This virtue typically involves:

- Sacrificial love
- Serving others without any reciprocal reward in mind
- A gracious attitude toward others which is seen through words and action
- Vulnerability, risking being humiliated or suffering at the hands of others
- Forgoing one's 'rights' for the sake of the wellbeing of others.

Because we are self-centred beings, it usually does not come naturally, although when entrenched in a subculture where it is valued, it can seem to be the natural thing to do.

It is a willing choice. It involves putting off pride and self-oriented thoughts and actions, and putting on selflessness and other-focused thoughts and actions.

This humility is not a purely personal thing. It is a life choice lived in relation to others. It is not the choice of a recluse or someone absorbed in themselves. It is lived in the context of a social setting. It is an approach to life in the midst of others, whether they be friends, neutral associates or enemies.

Humility is not an insipid acceptance of the unsatisfactory way things are. Rather, it often comes with a steely resolve to overcome. It can be exercised by a discontent – even an anger, not a bitterness from personal disappointment or shame, but an anger with the injustice or suffering someone else is experiencing. This humility is often the brother of courage.

Humility, my intended approach to Scripture

As I embark on examining the story and teaching of the Bible in relation to this topic; as I begin an exercise in interpreting the Bible, I need to approach this exercise with humility.

When reflecting on their practice, professional historians recognise this principle. Some reflective historians will say such things as:

- We are prone to use history for our own self-aggrandisement
- We should not stand above history, as we are subjects of our own historical background
- Do not use history to self-justify

- We need to submit to the true Lord of history and ask Him to give us knowledge of the truth about history and its relationship to us and what we should do
- We should be prepared to respond to history with humility, sorrow and even repentance.

How much more as an interpreter of the Bible should I embrace such an approach?

It is easy to come to the Scriptures with my idea of what they say and look for the passages and verses which prove my point. This is hermeneutical arrogance. I will not discover the truth this way.

Rather, I need to take a different stance – a stance of humility. I have confidence in the truth I know, but I do not assume I know the truth perfectly. I need to come to the Scriptures with an open mind. I need to submit to the Word rather than expecting the Word to fit into my ideas. If my preconceived ideas are blown apart, so be it. Humility demands that I be vulnerable to the possibility of being shown to be wrong, and that I may need to change my mind.

REFLECTIONS

A recipient of a prize is asked how they feel about the award. She answers, 'I am humbled.' What do you think she means? What other words instead of 'humbled' might they have used?

Why Humility Matters

Take a few moments to put into words what you understand humility to be. What is the underlying attitude? What does it look like? What do others see?

2

HUMILITY IN THE ANCIENT WORLD
THE COUNTER-CULTURAL NATURE OF HUMILITY

Humility in the ancient world

In the ancient cultures in which the story of the Bible is set, being proud was a virtue. As in many cultures both past and present, Greco-Roman society was dominated in many ways by an 'honour and shame' mentality. Social kindness and justice, personal pleasure, prosperity and knowledge were valued, but the most desired outcome of life's endeavours was honour. The goal of parenthood was that one's family brought you honour not shame. Leadership, whether political, military or domestic, was dominated by the objective of achieving honour through success. The goal of military conquests was to receive the accolades of the victory parade on returning home. Political leaders often developed a lust for fame and power. Alexander the Great, Julius Caesar, Herod the Great and Nero are just a few of the notable examples of this.

We have heard the expression 'self-praise is no recommendation'. That would have not resonated with the mindset of most ancients. It was not uncommon to publicly declare one's success. Many ancient chronicles were penned by the winners who had no compunction about lavishly recording their successes and only their successes. Boasting, even arrogance, was considered a virtue. Even better still was to get someone else to say how great you were. Of course you had to make sure that what you said about yourself was not blatantly false. That could 'come back to bite you'.

Honour could be gained by having the right connections, belonging to or in some way being associated with a prestigious social class or person. On the other hand, disgrace could come from being associated with the disgraced and the humiliated, such as imprisoned or executed criminals. Distancing from the humiliated reinforced their humiliation. Shame was the ultimate scenario to be avoided. Humility was not a choice. It was thrust upon someone by social class, ethnic identity or gender, or came about through misfortune. It was humiliation.

Approximately half the population were slaves, the working class. To be born to slaves was an humiliation to be endured. Usually a slave was bound to his master for the rest of his life. Sometimes a slave was educated to be able to fulfil his servant role. For example, his role may have been a private tutor, called a 'pedagogue', a financial manager, or a fighter/protector, called a gladiator. For slaves, life's goal was to achieve the comparative honour of the master's approval. Perchance, by some unlikely goodwill, the master might set a slave free. But, of course he needed work and so, if the master was kindly disposed to his slaves, the slave would most likely choose to remain in his service. He chose to be a 'bond slave'.

Dividing the population in another way to this was division based on gender. To be a woman was to be in a position of humiliation. As they were typically considered to be incapable of wisdom and hence were not afforded an education, women were not consulted. They were therefore considered only fit for the subordinate role of childbearing and service in the home. Women were not given a role in public life. It was generally exceptional for a woman to be mentioned in ancient chronicles. And when they were, it would be the family of significant leaders, such as the famed Cleopatra. Otherwise women were effectively non-persons.

You may have heard that the ancient Greeks invented democracy. In cities such as Athens, public life decisions were made by a meeting (ecclesia) of the general public rather than by a king or emperor. But most of the population were in positions of humiliation: under the age of eligibility, female or low-paid slaves. It was a small proportion of the population who had any say in civic affairs. It was a matter of honour to be in the ecclesia.

In the Roman Empire, it was a prestigious honour to be a Roman citizen. Roman citizenship was granted by birth or by special dispensation of the Roman authorities. It granted you privileges such as the special honour of a say in public affairs and a fair trial in a Roman court.

Consequently, 'nobody in their right mind' would choose the humiliation of taking on the role of a servant, a woman, or a child, or even stand alongside or defend an inferior. One may have chosen to show obeisance to a public authority as this might be a means to gaining favour and prestige. The concept of choosing to be completely humble in any way without guaranteed reward was not in the mindset of the people of the ancient world. It was very much counter-cultural foolishness. There wasn't even a word for this type of humility in ancient languages. The ancient Greek word *tapeinos*, and the Latin *humilitas* conveyed the idea of being low to the ground and to be put low. They were the word equivalent of humiliation.

So, where did this ideal of practical humility come from, and how did it develop? Read on.

REFLECTIONS

Think of a time in your life when you were subjected to humiliation. How did you deal with this being imposed on you? How did it affect your self-esteem? Would it have the same effect on you today?

Research the life of a famous ancient social or political leader. How did they show pride or humility? How did it affect their leadership?

Imagine being a person of a humiliated class in ancient society. Try to imagine the idea that this is the way it is meant to be and there is no alternative. How would you relate to a person of a different class or gender? Would it cross your mind to 'buck the system'?

3

HUMILITY IN ANCIENT ISRAEL
INTRODUCING 'THE GOD FACTOR'

The Hebrew word for humility, *anawa*, has a similar meaning to the Greek and Latin equivalents mentioned in the previous chapter. It generally means to be low, or to perceive oneself as low.

The most ancient of the Hebrew writings found in the Bible suggest that humility comes from being confronted by God. This is an integral part of the message of the book of Job. Job had been unwittingly prideful. He had thought he had the right to know everything including the reason for his suffering. In chapters 38-41 of Job, God reminds Job of His mind-blowing power and supreme greatness and Job's comparatively complete insignificance. Job needed to humbly repent of his presumption.

Knowing that there is a God who created everything that exists, and that we are merely part of His creation, is reason to be humble in relation to Him. Psalm 8 extols the greatness of God and then says: 'When I consider [the greatness of God's creation,] what is mankind that you are mindful of them?' (Psalm 8:3-4). We are just a blip in time compared to Him. We are but grass (Isaiah 40:6-8).

The humility of Moses

The story of Moses highlights his personal direct encounters with God, starting with his dramatic meeting with God in the burning bush. He was immediately confronted with the uncaused, timeless, infinite I AM. Chapter 12 of Numbers relates an occasion when Miriam and Aaron had an issue with Moses. They thought it was not right that God seemed to speak only through Moses. Then it says: 'Now Moses was a very humble man, more humble than anyone else on the face of the earth' (Numbers 12:3). The Lord goes on to explain to Aaron and Miriam that He reveals Himself to a prophet through visions and dreams, but with Moses He speaks face to face, clearly and not in riddles (verse 8). Moses was different in that he had personally met God.

The writer of Hebrews in the New Testament reflects on this connection between Moses' humility and personal confrontation with God. Speaking of Moses, he says in Hebrews 11:

> He chose to be mistreated along with the people of God rather than enjoy the fleeting pleasures of sin. He regarded disgrace for the sake of Christ as of greater value than the treasures of Egypt, because he was looking ahead to his reward. By faith he left Egypt, not fearing the king's anger. He persevered because he saw him who is invisible.

Personal confrontation with God engenders and builds humility.

The humility of kings

The historical parts of the Bible were unique among ancient writings because they tell the stories of heroes of Israel and the faith 'warts and all'. For most of the heroes of the Old Testament, humility did not come naturally. Many leaders of ancient Israel were arrogant, reflecting the normal mindset found in their world. Even those whom God used to convey His revelation had not necessarily yet learned to apply it in their own lives.

There were some prophets and kings who questioned their calling in the light of their humble position in relation to God. Examples include Jacob, Gideon, Saul, David, Solomon, Isaiah, and Jeremiah. None of these men lived consistent, humble lives. In fact, for some, their lack of humility was notable, but humility was seen when they were confronted by God.

The story of David illustrates this well. David was a warrior, like most who rose to power as king in those days. From his youth he displayed the courage to kill wild animals threatening the sheep in his care, and the confidence to tackle the Philistine giant. When commissioned to lead armies against the enemies of Israel, he was outstandingly successful. The adulating crowds chanted, 'Saul has slain his thousands and David his tens of thousands' (1 Samuel 18:7ff). King Saul took this as humiliation and from then on saw David as a threat to his sovereignty and sought to eliminate David.

David did not hesitate to visciously slaughter many in battle. But when he had the opportunity to kill Saul, he did not. For David, Saul represented God in that he was anointed by the prophet of God to be king. He refused to harm him because he humbly respected God.

After becoming king of Israel and conquering many enemies and bringing the nation of Israel to its zenith of power, he could have pridefully told everyone how great he was in establishing his kingdom, and maybe he did. But he was not consumed by self-centredness. He was more concerned about building a temple to the glory of God.

God spoke to him through the prophet Nathan, declaring that not only he but his descendants for generations after him would rule over Israel. David's response begins with the words: 'Who am I, Sovereign Lord, and what is my family, that you have brought me thus far? And as if this were not enough in your sight, Sovereign Lord, you have also spoken about the future of the house of your servant – and this decree, Sovereign Lord, is for a mere human!' (2 Samuel 7:18-19). He went on to say that he humbly accepted God's message.

Later, in his arrogance and self-satisfaction, David lusted after Bathsheba, another man's wife. He used his power to get this man killed in battle so that he could marry Bathsheba. Once again Nathan the prophet spoke to David. This time it was very sternly. 'This is what the Lord, the God of Israel, says: "...Why did you despise the word of the Lord by doing what is evil in his eyes?"' and many more words of condemnation and promises of judgment to now come upon him because of his sin (2 Samuel 12:7-9ff). David could have done what most kings of his time would do – kill this man who was shaming him in this way. But once again David knew that Nathan represented God, he responded to Nathan humbly: 'I have sinned against the Lord' (2 Samuel 12:13).

Like all of us, he was imperfect in his humility, but did respond humbly when confronted by God. He was humble before God and those who represented God.

Personal confrontation by God is a fearful thing. Knowing who God is and who we are in relation to Him makes us aware of our own fragility, vulnerability and powerlessness. We are subject to the just judgment of God. The fear of the Lord is a direct consequence of meeting with Him. This is being humble before God.

Proverbs and humility

The Psalms and Proverbs encourage humility and begin to speak of the fruit of this humility. Humility is a prerequisite for learning:

> The fear of the Lord is the beginning of wisdom, and knowledge of the Holy One is understanding (Proverbs 9:10).

> When pride comes, then comes disgrace, but with humility comes wisdom (Proverbs 11:2).

Pride leads to destruction while humility leads to honour:

> Pride goes before destruction, a haughty spirit before a fall. Better to be lowly in spirit along with the oppressed than to share plunder with the proud (Proverbs 16:18-19).

> Humility is the fear of the Lord; its wages are riches and honour and life (Proverbs 22:4).

> Pride brings a person low, but the lowly in spirit gain honour (Proverbs 29:23).

That honour comes in due course not from other humans but from God.

The message of the prophets about humility

God told Solomon that humility was a prerequisite for repentance and to national restoration and prosperity.

> If my people, who are called by my name, will humble themselves and pray and seek my face and turn from their wicked ways, then I will hear from heaven, and will forgive their sin and heal their land (2 Chronicles 7:14).

God promised to revive the humble in His due time.

> For this is what the high and exalted One says – He who lives for ever, whose name is holy: 'I live in a high and holy place, but also with the one who is contrite and

lowly in spirit, to revive the spirit of the lowly and to revive the heart of the contrite...' (Isaiah 57:15).

These are major themes of the latter prophets.

The prophets like Amos and Micah admonished people to live humbly before God. Humility begins there, in the presence of God. Amos confronted the prideful corruption of the people of Israel in his time, particularly those who used their position of leadership to promote themselves and abuse the already humiliated. Speaking of the duty of us all, Micah said:

He has shown you, O mortal, what is good, and what does the Lord require of you? To act justly and to love mercy and to walk humbly with your God (Micah 6:8).

As we read through the pages of the Old Testament we see many examples of men 'humbling' themselves before kings and leaders. This was not different to the behaviour of others in their world. The difference is seen when the people of Israel related to God. It was God who evoked humility and that humility was in their relationship with Him. It was before God that these kings bowed, but we do not see kings humbling themselves before the lowly. It seems that this dimension of humility was yet to come.

And the prophets hinted at where this was to be found. The Jews began to look forward to the arrival of an anointed deliverer, a messiah. The latter prophets spoke of this Messiah as a powerful authoritative king. But there were in these prophecies some counter ideas about this Messiah.

For example, Zechariah proclaimed:

> See your king comes to you, righteous and victorious, ... He will proclaim peace to the nations. His rule will extend from sea to sea and from the River to the ends of the earth.

But in the gap in the quote come these strange words:

> ...lowly and riding on a donkey, on a colt, the foal of a donkey (Zechariah 9:9-10).

One would have expected he would ride on a regal vehicle like a magnificent white horse. The coming Messiah would behave in a strangely humble manner. We suspect this would have been confusing or overlooked by the hearers.

Some prophecies about the Messiah were even more confronting on this matter. In Isaiah 53, for example, instead of a declaration of His mightiness, His power and receiving high honour, we read of Him:

> He shall grow up as a tender plant, and as a root out of dry ground. He has no form or comeliness, and when we see him there is no beauty that we should desire him. He is despised and rejected by men, a man of sorrows and acquainted with grief. And we hid, as it were, our faces from him. He was despised, and we did not esteem [honour] him (Isaiah 53:2-3).

And:

> He was oppressed and he was afflicted, yet he opened not his mouth. He was led as a lamb to the slaughter ... so he opened not his mouth (Isaiah 53:7).

In contrast to the expectation of the readers, this was clearly humiliation.

A totally new way of leadership, deliverance, power and influence was to be revealed.

REFLECTIONS

Read Isaiah 6:1-7. Contemplate who God is in all His majesty and glory.

How do you shape up in significance compared to Him?

Draw near to Him in your heart as you consider who you are in relation to Him. Experience the fear of the Lord. Let that experienced humility lead you to a renewed commitment to Him as Lord of everything in your life.

4

HUMILITY IN THE STORY OF CHRIST
FOCUSING ON HUMILITY IN THE GOSPELS

His incarnation

The story of Jesus Christ begins with the incomprehensible act of humility, God choosing to come to Earth in human flesh, the incarnation of God the Son.

We find it hard to comprehend the absolute majesty and glory of being the creator and sustainer of all that exists. We struggle to get our heads around the nature of His being. He knows everything. He has power over everything. He is present everywhere! The atoms jump at His command all the time everywhere. His greatness surpasses any measure in the universe. It has been said that the enormous size of the universe is a little taste of what it means to be 'God-sized'. He is the ultimate 'I am'. He existed before (if that is the right word to use) there was time. He created the potential for change which we now call energy and hence He created time. We have done our hardest to be ungrateful to Him, to not recognise

Him, to try to be independent of Him, besmirch His name, and pursue a path of self-promotion and self-destruction.

Who in His right mind would choose to become one of us and live in the hovel, the mess we have made of ourselves and His creation? Who would choose to live right in the middle of the very ones who hate Him? Who would choose to place themselves in such a place of vulnerability? One who loves us as His special creation.

This is the beginning of the amazing gospel (good news story) of Jesus Christ. The man Jesus was the personification of the incredible humility and sacrificial love of God. The Gospel writers Matthew and Luke clearly describe the humble circumstances of His birth. It was not just accidental humiliation. It was God's choice that He be born and spend His first days in an animal enclosure. It was true humility.

His ministry life

John the Baptist recognised who Jesus really was and said he was not worthy to even attend to Jesus' shoelaces. But Jesus submitted to being baptised by him to fulfil all righteousness. Fulfilling righteousness involved humble submission.

The story of the temptation of Jesus, soon after this, is related in Matthew chapter 4. It involves Him facing the temptation to use the power available to Him as God. Rather, speaking the Word of God, He drew upon the power of the Holy Spirit to resist. He was not about to invalidate His calling, to annul the humility of His incarnation.

The story of the ministry of Jesus is studded with examples

of acts of humility. With a few notable exceptions, His teaching did not specifically focus on His personal humility. He lived humbly rather than highlighting His humility (which of course would not be humble). He taught by action and words. Here are just a few examples of this, recorded in the Gospels.

The centrepiece of Matthew's story of Jesus' teaching, starting in chapter 5, is the 'Sermon on the Mount'. At the beginning of the sermon are the Beatitudes, the good attitudes that bring blessedness, being happily healthy.

> Blessed are the poor in spirit, …those who mourn, …the meek, …those who hunger and thirst for righteousness, …the merciful, …the pure in heart, …the peacemakers, …those who are persecuted (Matthew 5:3-12).

The words humble or humility are not specifically used here, but there is no doubt that true humility is a vital component of each of them. For example, the poor in spirit are those who honestly recognise that they are utterly destitute in relation to God. Those who mourn are those who sorrowfully regret their sin and are thus led to repent. These first two Beatitudes signal the lowliness of spirit and self-esteem, the conviction of sin that leads to the sorrow of repentance. These are the first steps on the path to being in a position of peace with God within oneself and then to practise humility. The meek are those who hold back their power and prestige when under pressure to intimidate or control others. Those who hunger for righteousness are those who recognise their own unrighteousness and desire to be made right, and who recognise and desire justice for those who endure injustice. The merciful are those who are willing to forgive rather than inflict revenge. The peacemakers risk danger and their own lives to bring about reconciliation. These attitudes are all counter-intuitive or counter-cultural and all involve some aspect of humility.

Jesus goes on to teach that kingdom living is all wrapped up in 'the law of love' which fulfils the 'law and the prophets' of the Old Testament. He emphasises the counter-cultural nature of life in the kingdom of heaven.

> You have heard it said… but I tell you … love your enemies, and … go the second mile… (Matthew 5:17ff).

These were practical life choices involving humility. They were clearly confronting the cultural norms of the day.

He teaches about humility in the way we do acts of charity such as giving to the poor and the way we pray.

> When you give alms, don't let your left hand know what your right hand is doing, that your giving may be in secret… (Matthew 6:3ff).

This curious reference to the left and right hand is about pride and humility. The ancients considered the right hand to be 'righteous' and the left to be 'evil'. He was saying, don't let the self-seeking prideful side of our nature gloat about and celebrate the good things we do. It is God, not we, who should receive the glory. So He said, do good humbly, without a public show.

On numerous occasions, Jesus engaged with women and

non-Jews in conversations about important matters. In the light of the prevailing attitudes, these were counter-cultural acts of humility. One of these occasions was His interaction with the woman at the well, related in John 4. She was a Samaritan, a woman, and an object of abuse in her community, and yet He spoke to her about deep spiritual things. Then there was the woman who came on behalf of her sick daughter, related in Matthew 15. She was a Canaanite, and her conversation with Jesus demonstrated she was prepared to accept the humiliation of being considered a 'Gentile dog'. Jesus healed her daughter immediately.

Jesus' humility led Him to go without many things in life including the usual marks of honour that go with being a rabbi.

On one occasion Jesus was eating at a prominent man's house. Part of the story in Luke 14 reads:

> When he noticed how the guests picked the places of honour at the table, he told them this parable: 'When someone invites you to a wedding feast, do not take the place of honour, for a person more distinguished than you may have been invited. If so, the host who invited both of you will come and say to you, "Give this person your seat." Then, humiliated, you will have to take the least important place. But when you are invited, take the lowest place, so that when your host comes, he will say to you, "Friend, move up to a better place." Then you will be honoured in the presence of the other guests. For all those who exalt themselves will be humbled, and those who humble themselves will be exalted.'

The point of the story seems to be that prideful acts of self-promotion can make us vulnerable to humiliation, but true humility is rewarded, if not in this life, then in the kingdom to come. He went on to recommend that a host invite the poor, the crippled, the lame and the blind, those unable to repay, that is, to bless the humiliated. In due course, one would be repaid in the resurrection of the righteous.

Jesus told the story of a prideful religious person and a humble tax collector. The Pharisee thanked God that he was not a despised tax collector, while the tax collector beat his chest and said, 'God have mercy on me a sinner.' Jesus went on to say:

> I tell you that this man, rather than the other, went home justified before God. For all those who exalt themselves will be humbled, and those who humble themselves will be exalted (Luke 18:14).

When the disciples asked Him who would be the greatest in the kingdom of heaven, He drew their attention to a child and said that, unless they changed in their attitude and became like children, they wouldn't even enter the kingdom. Jesus continued:

> Therefore, whoever takes the lowly position of this child is the greatest in the kingdom of heaven. And whoever welcomes one such child in my name welcomes me (Matthew 18:4-5).

When James and John wanted to be given positions of glory in God's kingdom, the other disciples were displeased with them. Jesus taught them:

> You know that those who are regarded as rulers of the Gentiles lord it over them, and their high officials exercise authority over them. Not so with you. Instead, whoever wants to become great among you must be your servant, and whoever wants to be first must be slave of all. For even the Son of Man did not come to be served, but to serve, and to give his life as a ransom for many (Mark 10:42-45).

Luke 22 records a similar (or possibly the same) occasion. Jesus taught by word and deed that true greatness involves humble service and self-sacrifice.

At the Last Supper, Jesus illustrated this lesson by taking on the pose of a servant and washing the disciples' feet (John 13). John introduces his account of this act by saying that Jesus knew His identity as God. True humility is not having a low opinion of yourself, but rather having accurate self-knowledge and choosing to act humbly.

His crucifixion

The ultimate focus of the gospel of Jesus is the story of His Passion. Each of the Gospels has the story of His suffering and death as the climax of their story. The crucifixion is the whole point or purpose of the life of Christ. The humility of the incarnation was to purposefully culminate in His death and subsequent resurrection.

Crucifixion was the most excruciatingly painful and humiliating punishment that the Romans could inflict on a person. It was reserved for the lowest of the low, the most hated by the state, the absolute antithesis of the honour that all citizens desired. It was to be avoided at all costs. Yet the Gospel writers tell the story of Jesus who set Himself to go to Jerusalem and put Himself in the position where they would inflict it on Him. The anticipation of it brought great agony. He sweated drops of blood in anticipation. But for the sake of what it would achieve for others, He was determined to follow it through.

The death of Christ was the ultimate act of humility that would change the whole course of human history. The disciples of Christ reflected on this and it changed their whole purpose in life, and it changed their mindset in relation to honour and shame, as the rest of this book relates.

REFLECTIONS

Read Matthew 5:1-12 again.

Have you stepped through the experience of the first two Beatitudes? Have you come to terms with your spiritual destitution and sinfulness before God? Have you then repented before God of your sin and thrown yourself on the mercy of God to lift you out of despair and into the joy of trusting in Jesus? Talk to God about this and then tell others about it.

5

THE PRACTICE OF HUMILITY
AS TAUGHT IN THE EPISTLES

The instructions we read in the Epistles about how to live the Christian life, about the way we relate to others, and about the relationship of slaves to their masters, citizens to governing authority, wives to their husbands, husbands to their wives, and children to their parents, must be seen in context – both in the letter in which it is written and in the cultural context of the New Testament times.

These instructions are often found in the practical teaching part of the epistle which comes after the doctrinal part of the epistle, after the teaching about what Christ has achieved for and in us.

In Romans

The first chapters of the letter to the Roman Christians, the main part of the letter, spell out the good news that Paul preached everywhere he went. It explains that we are made right with God not by our works and trying to keep the rules but by trusting in the work of Christ. We are made righteous by believing in Him. This is the liberating truth that was rediscovered 500 years ago in the Reformation. We conquer sin and death by faith in His conquering of sin and death and by the power of His Spirit.

The latter part of Romans begins in chapter 12 with:

> Therefore (in the light of the previous teaching of our righteousness in Christ and our walk in the Spirit) ... this is how to live your lives as followers of Christ.

In verses 1 to 3 he urges three fundamental starting points to living the Christian life:

> 1 ...offer your life sacrificially. This is deliberately humbling ourselves before God and humbly doing everything we do for God.

> 2 ...renew your attitude of mind. This is the humility of thinking, the teachability that enables us to unlearn the attitudes and thoughts that we have absorbed from the culture of the world, repent and learn the thought patterns of Christ.

> 3 ...don't think too highly of yourselves. This is humble self examination to accurately discern our God given personal strengths which God has given us so that we can serve.

At the core of each of these three instructions about the way to embark upon practising the Christian life is humility.

And then Paul continues in the rest of chapter 12 and the following chapters to outline how to practise sacrificial love. Although in detail it may look different, for each one of us it is the same 'law of love'. Here is a sample of phrases found in these chapters, illustrating that our life choices are to be about sacrificial love and humility:

- let your love be sincere
- love one another, showing honour to one another
- contribute to the needs of others
- don't be high-minded, but associate with the humble
- be subject to civil authorities
- owe no-one anything except to love
- let us not judge one another but rather not cause others to fall
- if your brother is grieved because of your food, you are not walking in love
- let each of us please his neighbour for his good, leading to edification
- receive one another.

Through Paul, God clearly tells us that the essence of the ongoing Christian life is humble service, sacrificially loving others. Just as Christ did not live to please Himself, we too should not live to save and serve ourselves.

> May the God who gives endurance and encouragement give you the same attitude of mind toward each other that Christ Jesus had… (Romans 15:5).

In Galatians

Galatians may well be the first of the letters in the Bible penned by Paul. In it he addresses a very early concern that arose in Gentile churches. They were being told by some Jewish believers that, to live out their lives in Christ, they needed to practise Jewish customs and laws, such as circumcision. They were being told to practise Judaism. These 'Judaisers' were actually giving religious justification to cultural arrogance. Paul is quite forceful in his condemnation of this practice, using expressions such as 'I marvel that you are so quickly removing from Him…' (Galatians 1:6 ASV), and 'O foolish Galatians, who did bewitch you…' (Galatians 3:1 ASV).

As he does in Romans, Paul explains that the purpose of the (Jewish) law is not to provide a means of salvation (wholeness) but to bring us to the Saviour, Jesus Christ. The law reveals we are all sinners and we all need the Saviour. Through faith in Christ, not by keeping the rules of the law, we are all made right with God.

> …there is neither Jew nor Greek, neither slave nor free, nor is there male and female, for you are all one in Christ Jesus (Galatians 3:28).

In the light of this, we go about living our life, not by focusing on keeping rules, nor by being led by our selfish desires (lust, works of the flesh), but by being motivated by love (selfless other-serving) and being guided by the Spirit (see Appendix 2). Love is our motivation, the ongoing purpose of acts of humility.

Throughout this letter, Paul reminds us that we share in the humility of the cross – 'I am crucified with Christ, nevertheless I live. Yet not I but Christ lives in me…' (Galatians 2:20). Keeping the law can be a prideful thing. Some are focused on keeping the law so that they may glory in the flesh.

> May I never boast except in the cross of our Lord Jesus Christ, through which the world has been crucified and I to the world (Galatians 6:14).

He concludes with, 'walk according to this rule' (Galatians 6:16). The 'rule' to live by is not legalistic law-keeping ('circumcision'), nor licence ('uncircumcision'), but rather the choice of humility and sacrificial love because we are new persons in Christ.

We all tend to favour the cultural forms we experience in our formative years. We can even give them religious justification, as some of the first generation of Jewish Christians did. It takes humility to recognise our own preferences, and it takes humility to address them when we are living in a bicultural or multicultural setting.

REFLECTIONS

Read Romans 12:3-8.

Romans 12:3 encourages self examination, to not think of ourselves more highly than we ought, but think soberly about ourselves. When you do this, do you like what you see?

This passage describes seven different gifts or unique motivations we may possess. We see in ourselves each of these in varying amounts. Under these seven headings, list ways in which they can be expressed with arrogance, and conversely with humility. Now examine your own personal life. How do you live out your personal calling?

In a group, look again at Appendix 2. Discuss how you have practically appropriated this way of life.

6

THE PRACTICE OF HUMILITY
FROM OUR POSITION IN CHRIST

The practice of humility, of lowering oneself for the sake of others, is only possible if we start from a position of dignity not shame. This humility presupposes an awareness of a position of dignity down from which we can choose to step. Arrogance, the opposite of humility, is often a manifestation of personal insecurity, while personal security and humility go hand in hand.

Knowing we are loved and valued by those we love is possibly the greatest factor in self-confidence and a positive self-esteem. Striving to achieve for the purpose of gaining the approval of loved ones is a recipe for despair. How much more if we desperately strive to gain the approval of God. The life of the 16th century Reformation leader, Martin Luther, illustrates this well. He desperately tried to do what would gain the approval of God. He tried 'everything' to appease his overwhelming sense of guilt. His heart was a morass of internalised humiliation. As a teacher of Scripture, he researched the New Testament. In the epistles of Paul, he discovered that only by trusting in the work of Christ on our behalf can we gain the acceptance of God. Martin Luther realised that humility was no longer a virtue that earned grace but a needed response to the gift of grace. This is the gist of much of the message conveyed in the epistles we have in the New Testament.

The first part of Paul's letter to the Ephesians classically spells out the idea that we no longer need to consider ourselves in a position of humiliation. Regardless of our exceeding sinfulness, regardless of our social status, regardless of our ethnicity or race, regardless of our gender or age, in Christ we are recipients of His grace, we are all children of God, we are all 'blessed with every spiritual blessing' (Ephesians 1:3), we are all seated with Christ 'in heavenly realms' (Ephesians 2:6). The word translated 'blessed' is the Greek word *eulogetos* from which we have the word eulogy. It means 'spoken highly of', or imparted with greatness and honour.

Here is a list of a few of the phrases found in Ephesians chapters 1 to 3, illustrating the nature of this 'blessedness':

- to the saints (holy ones) who are steadfast in Christ
- (God) has blessed us in Christ with every spiritual blessing in the heavenly realms
- He chose us to be holy and blameless
- to be adopted as His own children
- He lavished upon us every kind of wisdom
- we obtained an inheritance
- we were sealed with the Holy Spirit
- even when we were dead in our sins, He has made us alive together in Christ

- He has raised us up together and seated us in the heavenlies
- the immeasurable riches of His free grace toward us
- we are His handiwork recreated in Christ.

Paul said he was writing to the Ephesians and praying for them that they might practically realise this wonderful grace that surpasses understanding. We don't need to strive for status. We don't need to exercise self-promotion, because we already have exceeding greatness freely lavished on us.

This was all achieved by the sacrificial love, the humility of Christ on the cross, and His resurrection from the dead. Our position of honour is not achieved by our efforts of self-promotion, nor by our efforts to be humble, but is achieved by the work of Christ. There are no grounds for prideful boasting about this. Instead, we are encouraged to glory, not in our efforts, but in the cross, Christ's efforts on our behalf. He is exalted, and thus we are raised up in Him. What a wonderful position from which to confidently practise humility!

I am reminded of an occasion when Sir Edmund Hillary was being interviewed by someone about his service to the people of the Himalayas. He was the first man to scale Mount Everest, in 1953, when the equipment they had was quite primitive and clumsy compared to today. He was part of a team assisted by local helpers. Hillary went on to do other great exploits. He became a New Zealand national hero. In much of his later life he spent his energy serving others. With the same determination that he used to reach the top of Everest, he made personal sacrifices to improve the life of the people of the Himalayas.

He was rarely interviewed by the media, but on this occasion, later in his life, he was asked about his humility – why was he so humble? In reply he did not say he was not all that great. He did not put himself down. Instead, his reply with a smile was something like this: 'I guess I have a lot to be humble about.' He was saying in his typical low-key manner that he had achieved much. He knew that his success was a result of extreme courageous effort. He knew that his service to the people of the Himalayas came with much personal cost. He also knew that the acclaim he received was a challenge, a temptation to be puffed up about his success.

Just as Hillary told it like it is, we are reminded that humility is not a hypocritical putting down of yourself. It is rather soberly or accurately recognising who we are and choosing to not parade this reality, and quietly getting on with serving others. But unlike Hillary, our position of high acclaim is not a result of our achievement but rather the achievement of Christ. Hence it is indeed the cause of our attitude of humility. Our confidence in Him is the starting point for the Christian practice of humility.

Paul begins the second half of the letter to the Ephesians with the word 'therefore'. We are to live our lives in the light of our understanding of our position in Christ. What this looks like is described in the following chapters of Ephesians and is a major emphasis in the rest of this book.

REFLECTIONS

How do you feel about yourself? Do you have a sense of guilt, or shame, or self-satisfaction, or pride, or superiority? Do you have people in your life who put you down? Or do you have some who tell you that you are fantastic? Remind yourself that what you think about yourself should not be based on what others think of you but rather on what *God* says about you. Saying to yourself, 'I am who God says I am', re-read Ephesians 1-3.

How open are you to personal criticism? Does it evoke in you a reaction of pride? How can you overcome this pride?

7

THE PRACTICE OF HUMILITY
IN THE IMITATION OF CHRIST

Philippi was a Roman governmental centre in the region of Macedonia. Part of the culture of the citizens of the city was an awareness of the social privilege of Roman citizenship. Many Philippians were proud Roman citizens. Thus, the main theme of Paul's letter to the Philippians is the mindset of humility necessary to practise the Christian life of love in this context. Writing from the humiliating position of imprisonment in a Roman jail, Paul prays 'that (their) love may abound still more and more' (Philippians 1:9).

Chapter 2 is considered the focal point of the letter. Paul writes that if there is anything he wants of them it is that they be likeminded:

> ...let nothing be done out of selfish ambition or conceit, but in lowliness of mind let each esteem others better than himself... (Philippians 2:3-4).

And,

> Let this mind be in you which was also in Christ Jesus, who being in the form of God, did not consider it robbery to be equal with God, but made Himself of no reputation, taking the form of a bondservant... He humbled himself and became obedient to the point of death, even the death of the cross... (Philippians 2:5-8).

This letter is an exhortation to be humble in attitude and practice.

The rest of the letter begins with the familiar 'Therefore...' and encourages the readers to work this out in their lives 'with fear and trembling' (Philippians 2:12). Why fear and trembling? Not only were they living in the presence of the awesome Almighty, but it was a scary thing to be truly humble in practice. It involved the vulnerability of possible misunderstanding, rejection, derision and outright persecution, humiliation and possibly even death. Even if not physical death, the Christian life of humility involves death to self.

Paul continues by commending to them Timothy and Epaphroditus who are like-minded. He reminds them, with this humble mindset of not glorying in earthly things but rather in their heavenly citizenship in Christ – to doggedly press on.

> But whatever were gains to me I now consider loss for the sake of Christ. What is more I consider everything a loss because of the surpassing worth of knowing Christ Jesus my Lord, for whose sake I have lost all things. I consider them garbage that I may gain Christ and be

found in Him, not having a righteousness of my own that comes from the law, but that which is through faith in Christ... (Philippians 3:7-9).

Finally, he encourages them to not dwell anxiously on the negative, but to pray with thanksgiving, allowing the peace of God to guard their hearts, and to meditate on good things, and endure and achieve with the strength that Christ gives. He speaks of contentment in all circumstances. If we are content with who we are in Christ and His calling, we can risk humiliation as it does not affect our identity. It is no threat to our relationship with Him. Our confidence is in Him. I can do all this (endure whatever and wherever my choice to be humble takes me) through Him who gives me strength (Philippians 4:13).

In short, the book of Philippians urges us to recognise that Christ's subsequent exaltation was initiated by His humility. And His humility was built upon His knowledge of His identity as God. This is the example we are to follow. Knowing who we are in Christ, we can with determination live a life of sacrificial love with all humility.

The practice of humility is an integral part of living in the imitation of Christ.

REFLECTIONS

What aspects of the humility of Christ can you aspire to imitate?

Why Humility Matters

Read Philippians 3:7-9 again.

Think about things in your life that you cherish. What is it that previously used to be of value to you but now you have lost to gain Christ? Is God challenging you about some other things you value? Are you prepared to 'lose' them so that others will gain Christ?

8

THE PRACTICE OF HUMILITY
IN MARRIAGE

In the 1950s there was a popular song which went along these lines: Love and marriage go together like a horse and carriage. We would be hard-pressed to argue with the general idea that love is an integral part of a marriage relationship, but we may be wary of prevalent ideas about what kind of love is an essential part of marriage. In the Western world, we have observed that the love often considered essential for a marriage to endure is a kind of romantic love, a sense of being a soulmate, and that if that is lost, the marriage is dissolved! The Epistle to the Ephesians proposes an entirely different type of love to be at the core of a Christian marriage. It is a committed love that involves humility and sacrifice.

As noted earlier in this book, the first three chapters of Ephesians outline our blessings in Christ. In particular, Paul emphasises our unity in Christ, with Jews and Gentiles who were previously apart now brought together in Him. Then, the second three chapters outline what the outworking of this would look like in their everyday life in Ephesus.

Paul begins this part of the letter with:

> As a prisoner of the Lord, therefore, I urge you to live a life worthy of the calling you have received. Be completely humble and gentle, be patient, bearing with one another in love (Ephesians 4:1-2).

He continues with expressions such as:

> ...no longer live as the Gentiles do, in the futility of their thinking (Ephesians 4:17).

The world's way of thinking and doing is contrasted to the way of living in Christ. When referring to the way of the world, Paul references Adam, Eve and the Fall. When referring to life in Christ, he references the sacrificial love of Christ for those who are in Him, and so urges his readers to, for example:

- be kind and compassionate (Ephesians 4:32)
- live a life of love (Ephesians 5:1)
- be careful as you live (Ephesians 5:15).

Then, when he introduces specific instructions to different groups of people such as wives and husbands, slaves and masters, he says:

> Submit to one another out of reverence for Christ (Ephesians 5:21).

This is clearly the essential lead-in to the following instructions. Regardless of the social relationship, an attitude of mutual humility is needed. The instructions in the following verses must be seen as illustrating this principle. These instructions are describing what humility looked like for his readers.

And so he writes,

> Submit to one another out of reverence to Christ. Wives, submit yourselves to your own husbands as you do to the Lord… Husbands love your wives just as Christ loved the church and gave himself up for her (Ephesians 5:21,22,25).

Some editions of the Bible separate the beginning of the sentence in verse 21 from the following part of the sentence and so need to add the word obey or submit after the word wives. This tends to give the impression that only wives need to submit. As outlined previously in this book, the prevalent attitude toward women must be understood to grasp the significance of what this is saying. Women were excluded from life outside their role in the home. A husband was expected to lord it over his wife. It was dishonourable to do otherwise. The Christian gospel confronted the heart of this social expectation. Men and women are equal before the Lord. And so the instruction to men to love their wives sacrificially as Christ loved the church was challenging them to act in a way that could well incur humiliation.

Paul supports his instructions to husbands by comparing Christ's love relationship with the church, and concludes by saying:

> However, each one of you also must love his wife as he loves himself, and the wife must respect her husband (Ephesians 5:33).

This same mutual submission is invoked in Paul's letter to the Corinthians (1 Corinthians 7:4).

Just as in Christ we are 'one body', and so we love Christ as He loves us, so too in marriage we are 'one body' and so we love one another as ourselves. At the core of our relationship with Christ is His humble love for us and our commitment to Him. The bottom line of Christian marriage is not romantic love (as good as this is) but our commitment to humbly love each other as Christ loved us.

Over recent decades there has been discussion about traditional wedding vows in which the bride promises to obey her husband. Often in the light of modern egalitarianism, this has been removed from the vows. In the light of the teaching of Ephesians to submit one to another, an alternative idea would be that both bride and groom promise to obey or submit to the other. Mutual humility is a key to unity.

There is no room for forcefulness ('coming on' strongly) or controlling in an intimate loving relationship. Such behaviour is characteristic of lust or a misplaced sense of power. Humble submission to one another is an essential part of love.

I once heard the story of a pastor who came from his home country in Asia to attend a conference in America. At this conference one of the speakers was a woman Bible teacher.

The pastor approached the woman and asked her opinion on a personal problem. He said that he was unable to get his wife to obey him, even when he beat her. What advice did she have for him? She realised that if her advice was not to his liking he would disregard it as coming from a woman. Recognising that the cultural norms in this matter in his land had similarities to that in ancient Ephesus, she kindly recommended that he read the book of Ephesians, especially chapter 5, with humility and self-examination. He reported on a later date that this process had revolutionised his attitude and his relationship with his wife and released her into sharing in the ministry to the people of his church.

Whether we be men or women, we do well to do the same – read Ephesians chapter 5 with an attitude of humility, being humbly prepared to change our thinking and practice as God speaks to us.

REFLECTIONS

How do you practice humility in your family? As a daughter or son? As a mother or father? As a spouse? As an aunt or grandparent?

Do you demand that it be reciprocal?

Ephesians describes marriage as a picture of Christ's relationship to His people. With this in mind, which of these should be the core nature of your marriage? And which ones should not be there at all? Romantic love? Commitment love? One-way submission? Mutual sacrifice and submission?

9

THE PRACTICE OF HUMILITY
IN CONTRAST TO FALSE HUMILITY

In the AD 400s near Aleppo in Syria, one could observe a man living on a platform on the top of a pillar more than ten metres high. His name was Simeon and he had been there living on a pole for 37 years. We can imagine this life of 'humility' was quite a 'tourist attraction'.

In the century before this, Christianity had moved from being a movement of people who were misunderstood, despised and humiliated to being the official religion of the Roman Empire. Now it was socially advantageous and even necessary, the honourable thing to be a Christian. Previously, to be a Christian and to be baptised had been a hard choice of humbling yourself before God, identifying with the death and burial of Christ. To have been baptised was now becoming a mark of honour. By and large, the official church was beginning to lose sight of the basic message of the gospel, the message of being righteous by faith in the work of Christ on the cross.

Some began to believe the path to righteousness was achieved through a life of personal deprivation. This move to a life of asceticism became more prevalent at this time. Some who became monks withdrew from the world and denied themselves any comforts including the basics of good food and healthy accommodation.

Simeon was an ascetic who decided to live his entire life on a platform up in the air. He had to have higher and higher columns to get away from the crowds who came to see him, and perhaps catch some of his holiness. When he died after life on a pole for 37 years they had to remove his emaciated body and dismantle the column. Others copied his behaviour. They became known as Stylites, after the Greek word *stylos* meaning 'pillar'.

The 'humility' of asceticism is not taught in the Bible. Asceticism is not sacrificial love in action. It is quite self-centred. It is focused on achieving personal holiness, on impressing God by humility. It is self-righteousness. It is false humility. Paul's letter to the Colossians addresses the false doctrine underpinning this practice of false humility.

Right from the first generation of believers in Christ, there were those who began to entertain ideas contrary to the core understanding of who Christ is and what we should do to embrace His salvation. These ideas seem to have come from the Greek cultural view of the world. At the core of these Greek ideas was the concept of the separation of physical reality, in particular our bodies, from metaphysical reality, the world of ideas. These ideas may be moral ideals, spiritual beings or our spiritual nature. These followers of Christ began to take on the idea that the physical reality, the world and our bodies are evil by nature and must be totally separated from the most holy and good God. This posed a problem with their understanding of who Jesus was. How could God become a human being in human flesh? He must be a product of an emanation of God (or a chain of emanations), not God Himself. And then we have the question of how His death could achieve total spiritual salvation. Salvation became a matter of their understanding or knowing particular ideas about spirituality, and a matter of denying their bodies of any pleasure. The degree of their holiness became measured by the amount of their knowledge and the amount of their self-denial. So they would be proud of their superior spirituality, their knowledge and their asceticism (self-denial). In other words, they would be proud of their 'humility'!

It would seem that some of the believers at Colossae were taking on something of these ideas and practices. We deduce this from the content of Paul's epistle to them. His prayer for them includes phrases such as '[may God] fill you with the knowledge of His will' and '[may you] grow in the knowledge of God' (Colossians 1:9-10). He was not denying the value of knowledge per se, but questioning the source and correctness of their knowledge and the place of knowledge in their salvation.

In the first chapter, Paul gets straight into his main point. Jesus is the Son and the Son is the image of the invisible God, the firstborn over (originator of) all creation.

> For in him all things were created: things in heaven and on earth, visible and invisible, whether thrones or powers or rulers or authorities; all things have been created through him and for him. He is before all things, and

in him all things hold together... But now he has reconciled you by Christ's physical body through death to present you holy in his sight, without blemish and free from accusation... (Colossians 1:15-23).

He confronts their error front on. Christ is God Himself and our salvation is achieved by His physical death and we are made holy by trusting in Him.

Supporting his argument, Paul speaks of himself as a suffering servant of the gospel. He says he suffered for their sake, 'to present to you the Word of God in its fullness' (Colossians 1:24-27). He hints that his humble service is an example for them.

In chapter 2, he warns them about philosophies based on human presuppositions rather than on Christ.

> For in Christ all the fullness of the Deity lives in bodily form, and in Christ you have been brought to fullness (Colossians 2:9).

Our salvation, our wholeness, our complete fulfilment is not achieved by our efforts, or by our acquisition of knowledge or by our acts of humility. Our fullness is found in the fullness of Christ in us. He then speaks about circumcision and baptism. Our righteousness is not achieved by the mutilation of the flesh or any outward acts of humility, but by our trust in, and our identification with the righteous work of Christ on the cross, the ultimate act of humility done for us.

Then he writes, 'Therefore...' (Colossians 2:16). Thus begins the practical instructions about how to live.

He warns against being puffed up with the notion of having superior knowledge. He warns against those who have a pride in their humble way of life.

> Therefore do not let anyone judge you by what you eat or drink, or with regard to a religious festival, a New Moon celebration or a Sabbath day (Colossians 2:16).

> Do not let anyone who delights in false humility and the worship of angels disqualify you. Such persons ... are puffed up with idle notions by their unspiritual mind. They have lost connection with the head ... why, as though you still belonged to the world, do you submit to its rules... These rules which have to do with things which are all destined to perish [external cultural and physical forms] ... with their self-imposed worship, their false humility and their harsh treatment of the body ... lack any value in restraining sensual indulgence (Colossians 2:18-23).

We are set free from the bondage of rules to achieve holiness. Rather, with our focus on the Lord, we put to death selfish desires and habits.

> Therefore, as God's chosen people, holy and dearly loved, clothe yourselves with compassion, kindness, humility, gentleness and patience. Bear with each other... forgive one another... and over all these virtues put on love... (Colossians 3:12-14).

When people look at us they see our clothes. What do others see in us? Do they see the love of Christ? Putting on compassion, kindness and humility is for the purpose of the good of others. If the purpose of an act of humility is to develop our personal spirituality, it is not true humility. Humility is the sacrificial part of love. When acts of humility are divorced from love, when humility is focused on self and not on the good of others, it is false humility.

It is love, not rigid rules, that overcomes lust. It is humility in the heart that comes from trusting in the work of Christ who humbled Himself that saves. This is where true humility and sacrificial love fit into our life in Christ. And this is what it looks like, what others will see, in our day to day life. For wives, husbands, children, parents, slaves, and masters, the attitude of compassion, kindness, humility, gentleness and patience is the same, and the practical instructions vary according to their role in their society.

> Wives, submit yourselves to your husbands, as is fitting in the Lord.
>
> Husbands, love your wives and do not be harsh with them.
>
> Children, obey your parents in everything, for this pleases the Lord.
>
> Fathers, do not embitter your children, or they will become discouraged.
>
> Slaves, obey your masters in everything, and do it … with sincerity of heart and reverence for the Lord.

Whatever you do, work at it with all your heart, as working for the Lord...

Masters, provide what is right and fair, because you know that you also have a Master in heaven (Colossians 3:18-4:1).

These instructions are not rigid rules to be adhered to, but rather a description of what the practice of humility and love looks like. Regardless of our position in the family or society, the outworking of our fullness in Christ involves humility of the heart toward God and each other, along with a commitment to prayer and conversations with outsiders full of grace.

The practice of humility is not asserting our rights, nor denying ourselves of pleasures to achieve righteousness, but rather sacrificially loving others. Throughout the history of Christianity, there have been some who have chosen to live lives of asceticism – denying themselves of anything pleasurable in life. It is not for us to judge others for their actions as it is God, not us, who can see their motives. We can, however, examine our own motives. We can ask the questions: Is my 'humility' self-denial to achieve something for myself, or is it a means to loving others? Is my 'humility' drawing attention to myself, or drawing others to Christ? Is my humility true or false?

Our life in Christ is not about 'humbly' submitting to rules, whether derived from the Bible (Old Testament or New Testament) or derived from the philosophies of the world. But rather it is about accepting the grace of God in Christ and choosing action which flows out of humble sacrificial love for others.

REFLECTIONS

What is the purpose of fasting?

Is it an end in itself, or is it a means to equip us to better serve God and others?

How does it work?

How do you fast so that you are not drawing attention to yourself?

Should we tell others that we are fasting?

How does the instruction, 'masters provide what is right and fair, because you also have a Master in heaven…' work out in a modern business employer/employee relationship?

10

THE PRACTICE OF HUMILITY
IN CHRISTIAN COMMUNITY

The First Epistle to the Corinthians addresses issues of conduct in the context of the local church fellowship. Relational humility in contrast to arrogance and contention is a recurring theme in this epistle.

Written by Paul, this letter was one of a series of letters to the Corinthian Christians. In the ongoing conversation he addresses specific issues and attitudes that they had brought from their previous life into their Christian life. Thus, the details of his instructions are not necessarily universal rules of action. To view them as such would be petty legalism on our part. But rather, we need to discern the underlying eternal principles to be outworked in the context in which we find ourselves.

In the first chapters, Paul addresses the issue of prideful divisiveness. Reflecting the Greek culture in which they lived, some were claiming to have superior wisdom. He reminds them that they should glory only in Christ and identify with His cross:

> He who glories, let him glory in the Lord (1 Corinthians 1:31).

This was so counter-cultural as it was a disgrace in their culture to be associated with an executed criminal!

Others were claiming to follow a superior apostle, Apollos, Paul or Peter. Paul asserts that each apostle is humbly doing his part in building on the foundation of Christ. A serious factor in the rise of Christian factions (denominations or sects as they have been called) is the prideful attitude that we (the followers of our specific leaders) have a better handle on the truth than others. We need to have the humility to accept the possibility that this may not be true.

In chapter 4, Paul relates how he did not live for human approval. It is God who sees the heart, who is the judge, the One to whom we are accountable. Our self-respect is found in Christ in us, not in the honour others give us. Paul commends the risk of being considered fools for Christ's sake (1 Corinthians 4:10). He advocates intellectual humility.

He addresses other issues of morality and legal disputes. It would seem that some were taking their brothers to court to deal with disagreements, rather than resolving the issues themselves with meekness. Paul reminds them that this behaviour disregards what others will read into it. The possible loss of face and property by taking a course of humility and practising a disposition of forgiveness is better than publicly shaming the name of Jesus!

He addresses behaviour which could be construed as idolatory. The issue of what to do about food which had been previously offered to idols is an example. He points out that food is food – neither eating or abstaining is necessarily right or wrong. Our choices should stem from a motivation of love – the good of others, not ourselves. Others read and interpret our words and actions. Do our actions lead others to rightly see Christ? Our choice of action may involve humbly forgoing things which are in question and choosing otherwise so that God is glorified.

The issue in chapter 11 is their attitudes toward each other when they came together. He speaks of the message they gave to each other by the clothing they wore, and then by the way they conducted themselves during 'the Lord's Supper'. In both cases it seems there was an attitude of disrespect toward the other. It seems that women who had received the message that they were one in Christ with men thought that they now should behave like typical men in their culture – be haughtily proud, not submit to authority, bicker with one another and hog the oratory. They hadn't got the message about living a life of humility. They showed their attitude, their lack of humility, by breaking the cultural norms concerning modest, gender-appropriate clothing.

Paul begins this chapter by commending the Corinthians for holding on to the traditional teaching they had received from him.

> Follow my example as I follow the example of Christ. I praise you for remembering me in everything and for holding to the traditions just as I passed them on to you. But... (1 Corinthians 11:1-2).

He does not specifically say what this 'traditional teaching' was. Was it the traditional Jewish cultural way of conducting themselves as women and men? Hardly, as he vehemently opposed the teaching of 'Judaisers' who wanted Gentile Christians to follow Jewish rules. Or was it the teaching that in Christ they were equally co-heirs of His grace? Most likely yes, because the next word is 'but' which suggests that what follows is an apparent contrast. Then, with that 'but', he proceeds to tell them, (regardless of their equality in Christ), to show respect for authority in the culturally appropriate way.

He firstly tells them that authority structures are God's plan, using the idea of origin (headship) as the reason for the existing order. In the culture of the day, covering the head (or not covering) conveyed a message about one's attitude toward authority. Thus he encourages them to show humble respect for authority by the way they cover or do not cover their heads. In their culture, to show humble respect, women covered their heads, and men did not.

In verses 9 and 10, he once again uses the idea of origin as a way of understanding the social order. One could say this is the way things are in Adam, in the world's natural and fallen culture. In Adam, authority is dominance and a male thing (see Appendix 1). Then he says:

> Nevertheless, in the Lord woman is not independent of man, nor is man independent of woman. For as woman came from man, so also man is born of woman. But everything comes from God (1 Corinthians 11:11-12).

We are now in Christ. In Christ our attitude is to submit one to another, serving one another in love.

Paul is saying that in Christ we are all equally responsible to submit to the authority of the Lord. Note the reference in verses 11 to 15 to the 'very nature of things'. Presumably he means the cultural common sense, the logic of 'natural' humanity which shapes non-verbal messaging, about what we do.

Paul concludes this discussion around head covering with:

> If anyone wants to be contentious about this, we have no other practice – nor do the churches of God. (1 Corinthians 11:16).

The real issue is clearly divisive contentiousness, the failure to have an attitude of humility and to communicate that attitude verbally and non-verbally, according to the cultural norms of the day. Humility is an essential factor to maintain the mindset of unity.

Next, Paul addresses the prideful manner in which they behaved toward each other when they gathered for communion. He admonished them with words such as

> …do you despise the church of God by humiliating those who have nothing? (1 Corinthians 11:22).

Not having an attitude of humility towards one another is described as not discerning the body of Christ (1 Corinthians 11:29). They were encouraged to examine their attitude.

Then he addresses the prideful use of the manifested gifts of the Holy Spirit. He urges them to humbly work together to assist one another to excel in what they do. The gifts of the Spirit and acts of charity are worthless if they are not used as an outworking of love.

When writing about the priority of love, he references humility when he writes:

> If I give all I posses to the poor and give over my body to hardship that I may boast, but do not have love, I gain nothing (1 Corinthians 13:3).

Love is the essential heart of all our acts of true humility.
When describing love, he writes:

> Love suffers long and is kind; love does not envy; love does not parade itself, is not puffed up; does not behave rudely, does not seek its own... Love never fails (1 Corinthians 13:4-8).

Love is an attitude worked out in word and action, and clearly humility is an integral part of this love.

In chapter 14 he revisits the issue with instructions around the use of the vocal gifts of the Spirit in their meetings. Paul concludes that it is the Lord's command that everything be done in a fitting and orderly way. Arrogance and competitiveness breed confusion and conflict. Humble mutual submission brings the peace of unity.

> For God is not the author of confusion, but of peace, as in all the churches of the saints (1 Corinthians 14:33).

He reminds them to be humble because the Word of God did not originate with them but with God. People read non-verbal communication through a cultural filter. Let it not be said of us that our arrogance, expressed verbally or non-verbally, speaks more loudly than our acts of love.

The message of 1 Corinthians is clear. Christian church life is about humbly loving one another, not bragging about our superiority. It is about humbly forgoing our social rights so that others see and hear the message of Christ. It is about honouring one another, building one another up, and humbly submitting to each other in both word and deed.

REFLECTIONS

Why did you choose the particular local church of which you are a part?

Was it one or more of these?

- It is superior in some way to others, e.g. in music or doctrine.
- It provides opportunity for me to use my gifts to humbly serve others.
- It humbly contributes to and supports the whole body of Christ in my city.

- It makes me feel comfortable.
- It preaches the Word that builds me up in Christ.

Which of these do you think Paul encourages in 1 Corinthians?

What do you do to contribute to the ministry of your local church? How does humility shape your part in the body of Christ?

11

THE PRACTICE OF HUMILITY
IN LEADERSHIP AND THE WORKPLACE

A lecturer and some students at a Christian teacher education institute were having a conversation. A soon-to-graduate student raised an issue with the lecturer. It went something like this:

'I can't seriously follow the Bible when it blatantly promotes sexism and slavery.'

'What do you mean by that?'

'The Bible commands slaves to obey their masters.'

'You know what? If I were a Christian slave, I would do well to gladly serve my master. And, by the way,' she added with a smile, 'when you become a teacher in a school next year, you would do well to submit to your principal's leadership. I call it practical service shaped by Christian humility.'

'Oh, I never looked at it that way before.'

Most of us understand the need for humility in the role of the follower, but sometimes it seems more challenging to comprehend the part humility plays in leadership.

A few years ago a young Australian moved into local politics. He became the deputy mayor of a local suburban council. To celebrate his engagement to be married, he organised a party at his home. He ordered for the street outside his house to be free of traffic for the occasion. Understandably other users of the street complained. When questioned by the media he retorted, 'Don't they know who I am?' This blatant lack of humility marked the beginning of the end of his political career. Hopefully he learned that effective leadership involves humility.

Leaders as image bearers

God created us in His image and likeness. He is sovereign Lord over all His creation. He has dominion over everything. Thus He created us to be like Him. God created us to be managers, to take dominion of the environment in which He placed us (Genesis 1:28). He called us to manage the plant and animal life of the Earth. To help us do this, He built within us a sense of responsibility towards our environment, a sense of needing to care so that we all may flourish.

When Adam and Eve sinned they brought a curse on the human race (see Genesis 3). For example, weeds would become an issue. Instead of learning their value, we have just tried to control and eliminate them. Part of the curse of the fall was a strained relationship between men and women. And that strained relationship would be expressed by a controlling relationship, Adam controlling Eve (Genesis 3:16).

All of us in some way or other have misapplied our God-given sense of responsibility. We have used it to control our fellow human beings. We all need to examine ourselves in regard to this, particularly if we find ourselves in a leadership role. When this tendency becomes a dominant drive, it is called lust for power. It leads to a leadership culture of 'power and fear'. It stands in contrast to leadership characterised by humility. Sadly, as pointed out earlier in this book, the world has many people who think some form of self-promotion is an essential part of leadership.

The Bible has a radically different view of Christian leadership. Christ came to redeem us from the Fall. That includes saving us from our tendency toward dominating, controlling leadership.

When God exercises His control over creation, creation obeys. Without question, the stuff of matter obeys His laws. In contrast, when God exercises dominion over us who are made with a will like He has, He does it in a way that involves our will too. He is totally sovereign but does not control us like robots. Rather, He shapes our will to do what He has ordained to happen. As an old song says: 'He does not compel us, He makes us willing.' When we as image-bearers lead others, our leadership should be similar – not dominating and controlling, but inspiring and equipping others to follow.

When it comes to leadership, the New Testament describes behaviour that seems contrary to some of the accepted ideas of the time. For example, it is often overlooked that there are various references to women in leadership roles. Jesus started something new by His teaching about leadership. The first of the Beatitudes, 'Blessed are the poor in spirit, for theirs is the kingdom of heaven' (Matthew 5:3), implies that those who are in leadership in God's kingdom are the lowly of heart, not the arrogant.

How has Jesus the Master, the King of the kingdom led us?

- By teaching us His will
- By sacrificially, humbly serving us
- By equipping us with His Spirit
- By setting us free to do His will.

Leaders created in His image do well to imitate Him.

Servant leaders

As noted in a previous chapter, dominance is in the mould of Adam leadership. In Christ, leadership is submitting one to another, serving one another in love (see Appendix 1). Servant leadership is a term that is often used in Christian circles. There is a variety of ideas as to what it means in practice.

The story in John 13 of Christ washing the disciples' feet is often referred to in our understanding of Christian leadership. Christ took on the stance of a servant. He chose to assume a servant role; He humbled Himself in relation to those whom He led. John introduces Jesus' action by pointing out that Jesus knew that the Father had given all things into His hands (John 13:3). Jesus knew He had all authority. He knew He was the leader. Yet He chose to do the counter-cultural thing and acted with the pose of a humble servant, and washed their feet.

So when He had washed their feet, taken His garments, and sat down again [He assumed the cultural pose of the master teacher], He said to them, 'Do you know what I have done to you? You call Me Teacher and Lord, and you say well, for so I am. If I then, your Lord and Teacher, have washed your feet, you also ought to wash one another's feet. For I have given you an example, that you should do as I have done to you. Most assuredly, I say to you, a servant is no greater than his master, nor is he who is sent greater than he who sent him. If you know these things, happy are you if you do them' (John 13:12-17).

Do we get the message? Humility is an integral part of Christian leadership every day, not just as an occasional symbolic token gesture. The leader leads by humbly serving the team he leads.

In this vein, Paul in Ephesians 6:5-9, Colossians 3:22-25 and 1 Timothy 6:1-2, instructs servants (the ancient equivalent of employees) and masters (the ancient equivalent of manager/leaders and employers) to practise mutual humble service. Whatever our role, when we serve others we are indeed serving the Lord, and that we do with humility.

2 Corinthians

This letter to the church in Corinth was written in the context of some who arrogantly proclaimed themselves as 'super-apostles' and who challenged the apostolic leadership of Paul.

There was an incorrect model of leadership clouding the Corinthians' understanding of their life in Christ.

The letter is full of descriptions of suffering leadership, and what to 'boast' about. Right at the beginning of the letter Paul speaks of comfort in the face of suffering.

> Blessed be the God and Father of of our Lord Jesus Christ, the father of mercies and God of all comfort, who comforts us in our troubles, that we may be able to comfort those who are in any trouble, with the comfort with which we ourselves are comforted by God. For as the sufferings of Christ abound in us, so also our comfort abounds through Christ (2 Corinthians 1:3-5).

This theme of sharing in the humble suffering of Christ runs through the letter. The model of sharing in the suffering of Christ is particularly emphasised when Paul speaks of his own leadership which was being scrutinised and criticised.

Paul's competency as an apostle was being questioned. In chapter 3, he addresses this issue by saying that he was not seeking the confirmation, written or otherwise, of others in authority to prove his competence. Rather, he pointed out that their faith in Christ was the fruit of his ministry. His confidence was not based on the acclaim of others to boost his ego.

Not that we are competent in ourselves but our competence comes from God (2 Corinthians 3:4). It is God, not ourselves, who calls and equips the Christian leader. It is not for us to promote ourselves (see also 2 Corinthians 10:18). It is for us to humbly serve.

In chapter 4, in contrast to the deceptive arrogance of some, Paul speaks of his confidence in the face of his transparent weakness.

> We are hard pressed on every side, but not crushed, perplexed, but not in despair, persecuted, but not abandoned, struck down but not destroyed (2 Corinthians 4:8).

In chapter 6 he again describes in more detail such suffering (see 2 Corinthians 6:3-10). The humility of a Christian leader may expose him or her to criticism, emotional and even physical persecution. Vulnerability is an integral part of humility and this is particularly evident when one is in leadership.

In chapter 7 he commends them for their response to his reproof of them in a previous letter. They were humble enough to accept his correction and transparently to repent.

In the latter chapters of the letter, Paul describes and defends his leadership ministry. The enemy he faced was not the people whose practice was wrong, but rather their ideas, the attitudes that had ensnared their minds. It was these that he stood up against. These ideas promoted the authority of the person and not the lordship of Christ. Their attitude was not an attitude of obedience to Christ. It was the ideas and practice flowing from these arrogant ideas, not the persons themselves, that needed to be 'punished' (2 Corinthians 10:4-6).

Paul then goes on to speak, in chapters 10 to 12, of his apostolic authority. It was not to lord it over people, but to preach and teach the gospel in pioneering situations. He refused to make comparisons with other leaders, but rather to be confidently faithful to his calling, and to humbly minister, that is to serve. This included:

- Humbling himself so that they might be exalted and honoured because he preached God's gospel to them without expecting monetary payment. (See 2 Corinthians 11:7)
- Numerous and varied occasions of suffering for the sake of the ministry of the gospel
- Allowing people to see his weaknesses and his faltering manner of speaking.

Throughout this passage, he often uses the word 'boasting'. He says he is reluctant to boast, as it suggests self-promotion, the very attitude he is fighting against. But if need be, he would boast about (draw their attention to) his calling and his weakness, as these highlight the sufficiency and power of Christ.

In summary, in 2 Corinthians Paul taught that humility, not arrogance, characterised the true practice of apostleship. Humility is an essential part of effective Christian leadership.

The Pastoral Epistles

Timothy and Titus were assigned to pastoral roles. The letters to Timothy and Titus are often called the Pastoral Epistles. As such they give some insight into the practice of leadership.

On reading such verses as 1 Timothy 1:4, 1 Timothy 6:4, 2 Timothy 2:23 and Titus 3:9, it would appear that in the background of these letters was a context of arrogant intellectualism. Some purporting to leadership showed a sense of superiority as they engaged in speculative discussions, and promoted their high-minded ideas rather than using their speech to build others up. They were prone to promoting themselves as having a better grasp of the gospel and being more spiritual because of their superior knowledge.

In contrast, in 1 Timothy chapter 1, Paul offers a different model of leadership. He focuses on what good leadership in the church should look like. Leadership is about love. The goal of this command (Paul's instructions about his leadership) is love, which comes from a pure heart and a good conscience and a sincere faith (1 Timothy 1:5). Leadership is not about laying down the law on people, especially if they are 'the righteous', but rather involves teaching what is right by word and example (1 Timothy 1:8-11).

Leadership does not involve proving we are superior in knowledge and faith, but rather recognising our shortfallings and that our calling is solely through the grace of God (1 Timothy 1:12-17). A constant reminder (to oneself) that we are 'the chief of sinners', we are desperately sinful and that our righteousness is not of our own but of Christ, is an effective antidote to pride.

At times effective leaders, such as founders of large churches, are pressured by those who have benefitted from their leadership to sit proudly on a pedestal that their followers have made for them. If this is not resisted, the world will see the leader as an arrogant self-centred controller of people. If humility is not transparent, the leader will be accused of pride.

Our acts of mercy and our practice of humility are a response of gratitude for His sacrificial humility and mercy. Our good works are not of ourselves but rather of Christ in us. Paul clearly sees that he was saved, not to brag about his salvation or his apostolic calling, but to humbly serve his Saviour by serving others.

Unless the leader models humility, they have no persuasive power to ask those they lead to be modest, submissive and humble before God and others. In 1 Timothy 2, Paul urges Timothy to lead the people in this respect: to pray for all those in positions of authority, and to demonstrate humility before God rather than angry disputing. He urges the humility of modest dress, humble service (with good deeds) and learning in quietness and submission rather than asserting authority.

Women (possibly those aspiring to leadership) are addressed here, referring back to the attitude of Adam. Adam arrogantly shifted the blame and 'put the woman in her place' (see Appendix 1). This practice of keeping the women in a position of humiliation was prevalent in the Greco-Roman world in which Paul was speaking. Women were uneducated and expected to be subservient. Yet, in Christ, Christian women were told they equally shared in His blessings. So the apostle taught that, if they aspired to the role of teaching others, they should not push themselves forward to teach but rather humbly listen and learn before presuming to teach. Humility is a prerequisite to learning, and learning is a prerequisite to teaching.

One problem with recent feminism is not the defending of or the deferring to women (this is needful and right), but rather the promotion of immodest prideful behaviour, even female chauvinism, under the guise of 'assertive action'. All of us find it much easier to accept the leadership of others, male or female, if their leadership is exercised with humility.

In chapter 3, Paul outlines the desirable characteristics of those who could be chosen as overseers and deacons, the leadership of the local church. When one reads these, it is clear that the leader's authority is found in the respect he commands, the ability to teach and the example they give of how to live. Yes, characteristics of the humble, and not the arrogantly controlling, are seen in these lists.

It was not just Paul who taught this model of leadership. The apostle Peter, in the final chapter of 1 Peter gives similar instructions to leaders along this line:

> Be shepherds of God's flock that is under your care ... not pursuing dishonest gain, but eager to serve, not lording it over those entrusted to you, but being examples to the flock (1 Peter 5:2-3).

In chapter 4, Paul reiterates the encouragement to lead by instruction in the truth and by example, rather than by imposing rules. The imposition of rules is by nature inconsistent with living in the freedom of faith in Christ.

> Set an example for believers in speech, in conduct, in love, in faith and in purity (1 Timothy 4:12).

After a series of specific practical instructions, Paul finishes with an encouragement to steer clear of false teaching, prideful contention and the love of making money, but to pursue righteousness, godliness, faith, love, endurance and gentleness (1 Timothy 6:11).

In his second letter to Timothy, Paul writes about how to cope with false teachers. Paul says they are among those who are 'lovers of themselves, lovers of money, boastful, proud, abusive ... rash, conceited, lovers of pleasure rather than lovers of God' (2 Timothy 3:2-5). In contrast, he points to his own leadership:

> You know all about my teaching, my way of life, my purpose, faith, patience, love, endurance' (2 Timothy 3:10).

Good leadership is by example. It is intentional, resolute and humble.

In 2 Corinthians and the letters to Timothy, Paul is critical of leadership characterised by the opposite of humility – pride, contentiousness, self-promotion and legalistic control.

In contrast, he points to the example of his own leadership and his obedience to the call of God and willingness to suffer, if needed, to pursue that calling.

An arrogant and controlling leader generates disloyalty and divisiveness. Such a mindset is the seedbed of contention, controversy and war. Throughout history and globally, this has been the norm and servant leadership has been the exception.

The Christian leader should not be characterised by attitudes of command and control but rather by inspiration, service and facilitation. A humble leader commands respect and gains the loyalty of the team. It takes humility to withhold unnecessary control. Humility is a vital component in the character of a respected and inspiring leader.

REFLECTIONS

Research the life of King Oswald of Northumbria in the early AD 600s, and how he led his subjects to believe in Christ with the help of Aidan – St Aidan, apostle to Northumbria. How does their lifestyle and their method of evangelism reflect:

- an understanding of the nature of faith in Christ, and
- the use of humility to influence and lead people?

If you are called to leadership, take time to examine your attitudes and leadership style.

Have you taken the time to humbly listen and learn before presuming to teach and lead?

Do you tend to lead by example or by control? Do you inspire and release those you lead to achieve their goals, or do you tend to 'micromanage'?

12

THE PRACTICE OF HUMILITY
IN THE FACE OF OPPOSITION

The world was shocked by the images of the death of George Floyd in May 2020. George Floyd, a 46-year-old black American was seen saying, 'Officer, I can't breathe,' as his neck and head were being held down by the officer's knee. It was George's attitude of humility towards the officer that really stirred the conscience of millions of Americans and triggered massive demonstrations around the world. But when some demonstrators turned their protest into violence, a reverse reaction was evoked. Are there lessons to be learned from this?

How should we behave when our lives are threatened? How should we respond to abuse? Should we behave differently to normal, and fight back to defend ourselves? And how do we defend the faith when it is being challenged?

Peter was writing from Rome to believers in what is now central Turkey. This was at a time of persecution, of suffering at the hands of people in authority, because of their faith in Christ. In the light of the glorious hope and inheritance they had through the resurrection of Christ, he encourages them how to live – with sober minds set on the hope of the grace of Christ.

> As obedient children, do not conform to the evil desires you had when you lived in ignorance. But just as he who called you is holy, so be holy in all you do (1 Peter 1:13-16).

In other words, the attitude and practice of obedience (humility) should set us apart from the world from which we have come. Just as Christ is different (holy) so we should live a different (holy) life.

In the light of the fact that they were a chosen people, a holy nation, and thus foreigners and exiles in a pagan society, they were urged to live so that the world would see their radically different good life. How could they be different without offending the civil law? What would this look like in the given social order?

Chapters 2 and 3 of 1 Peter emphasise the attitude of submission to and honouring of others:

> ...submit to civic authorities, submit to your husband, honour your wife as a co-heir ... Submit yourselves for the Lord's sake to every human authority ... live as free people ... [free to] show proper respect to everyone, love the family of believers, fear God, honour the emperor (1 Peter 2-3).

Notice the purpose of this submission and respect was not to make themselves holy or to give themselves prestige, but rather for the Lord's sake. The purpose was to reflect the holiness of God in them, to bring honour to Him. This is choosing to be humble, to practise humility while representing Christ in the world.

He gives the same message to people in varying roles in society. To slaves he wrote,

> ...in reverent fear of God submit yourselves to your masters, not only to those who are good and considerate, but also to those who are harsh (1 Peter 2:18).

And to wives he wrote,

> ...in the same way submit yourselves to your own husbands so that, if any of them do not believe the word, they may be won over without words by the behaviour of their wives, when they see the purity and reverence of your lives. Your beauty should not come from outward adornment [bling, designer clothes and makeup]. Rather, it should be that of your inner self, the unfading beauty of a gentle and quiet spirit, which is of great worth in God's sight (1 Peter 3:1-4).

In the culture of the day, modest clothing invoked honour to the husband, and thus engendered respect to the wife. He points out that this is how women such as Sarah showed the beauty of the hope they had in God. They voluntarily submitted to their husbands. And then to husbands he wrote,

> ...in the same way [with humility by choice] be considerate as you live with your wives and treat them with respect as the weaker partner [socially disadvantaged, lacking in social status and opportunity as was the case in that society] and as heirs with you of the gracious gift of life (1 Peter 3:7).

Recognising his wife's equality in the Lord – in practice, by his attitude and action – was a huge challenge to the man of his time. It required humility.

Summarising this part, Peter wrote,

> Finally, all of you, be like-minded, be sympathetic, love one another, be compassionate and humble (1 Peter 3:8).

Peter then addresses behaviour in relation to those who threaten and humiliate. He instructs his readers to:

> ...do good ... even if you should suffer for what is right, you are blessed. 'Do not fear their threats; do not be frightened.' But in your hearts revere Christ as Lord. Always be prepared to give an answer to everyone who asks you to give the reason for the hope that you have. But do this with gentleness and respect (1 Peter 3:13-15).

The Practice of Humility – In the face of opposition

These instructions are most apt in the light of the polemic of vocal (and quite arrogant) atheists whose arguments amount to attempts to humiliate Christians.

It is clear that asserting our rights will drive people (in the home and in the community) away from, rather than drawing them to, our faith in Christ. On the other hand, Peter was saying that, in a society where power and intimidation were common, it was possible to influence the source of threats by the example of gracious humility.

Humility affects the heart of those involved. It can cut across social conditioning, the cultural 'common sense' or prejudice, and create change for good. Voluntary humility is an effective tool of a change agent. Sacrificial love is an effective tool of evangelism. In other words, our humility is not only a correct response to the grace of God in Christ but also an effective means of confirming the message of Christ in the world.

In chapter 4, Peter continues to encourage the readers to choose to live, not in selfish lustfulness, but with humility, choosing suffering for doing good. He includes these words:

> Therefore, if Christ suffered in his body, arm yourselves also with the same attitude [voluntary humility or even humiliation]…
>
> They are surprised that you do not join them in their reckless wild living, and they heap abuse on you…
>
> Each of you should use whatever gift you have received to serve others…
>
> Rejoice in as much you participate in the suffering of Christ… (1 Peter 4:1-13).

If, as the proverb says, a soft answer turns away wrath, how much more can humility assuage anger in the face of abusive opposition?

In the final chapter, Peter gives instructions to leaders along this line:

> Be shepherds of God's flock that is under your care ... not pursuing dishonest gain, but eager to serve; not lording it over those entrusted to you, but being example to the flock...
>
> In the same way, you who are younger, submit yourselves to your elders (1 Peter 5:2-5).

As noted in the chapter on leadership, humble leadership persuades by example, and those you lead will find it easier to submit to your leadership.

Peter summarises his letter with instructions such as:

> Yes, all of you be submissive one to another, and be clothed with humility, for 'God resists the proud, but gives grace to the humble'. Therefore, humble yourselves under the mighty hand of God, that He may exalt you in due time, casting all your care upon Him, for He cares for you (1 Peter 5:5-7).

1 Peter teaches us how to behave in the face of opposition, when the community at large is giving us a hard time. That community is observing us. They are observing more than how we react with them. They are observing how we live with

one another. This letter of Peter's is not about defining the roles of citizens, slaves, masters, women, men, and leaders, but about how to exercise humility in these roles, in both private and public life, and thus be an example of Him to each other and the world.

The message of Peter is that humility and sacrificially loving one another is not to be abandoned when facing opposition, but rather it is even more apt to live in this way. It effectively gives glory to God and truly reflects the person of the Lord Jesus Christ. Another apostle, John, recorded the words of Jesus after He humbly washed His disciples' feet:

> By this everyone will know that you are my disciples, if you love one another (John 13:35).

In the years that followed the writing of the New Testament during the time of the Roman Empire, followers of Christ were subjected to periods of severe persecution. Just as Peter reflected, the world did not understand their different humble life and their commitment to Christ in the face of enormous pressure. They were falsely accused, abused and often killed.

It was their enormous humility and sacrificial love that drew observers to seek Christ. Submitting to the humiliation of martyrdom was the most powerful expression of and witness to the grace of Christ. In time, the humility of the saints conquered the Roman Empire!

As we suffer by taking the path of humility, it may appear to the world that we are losing the battle. But, just as the death of Christ appeared at the time to be a lost battle, it was and is in fact the means to the final victory. The best form of defence is … humility.

In situations of conflict, whether international, local or within family, the best approach is often counterintuitive.

It is not arrogance. That provokes conflict.

It is not tolerance, in the sense of bland affirmation of all viewpoints.

It is not surrendering our convictions or our beliefs about the truth. It is about honouring those who have views different to yours – not for their views, but recognising their humanity and sincerity.

It is not about winning the argument, but about winning the peace – peacemaking, even if it may cost you your reputation or your life.

It is the practice of humility.

REFLECTIONS

How do you react to bullying or aggressive resistance aimed at you personally?

If appropriate, share your experiences in the group.

How do you encourage yourself?

Do you love and pray for the persecutor?

Discuss ways that you might convey to them the love of Christ.

13

THE PRACTICE OF HUMILITY
IN OUR LIVES

The letter written by James is a practically oriented book. It is often compared to wisdom books such as Proverbs. It has many succinct exhortations about how to live in everyday life. It focuses on practical issues such as enduring in trials, relating to the poor and the use of wealth, controlling our words, and living in community.

It repeatedly emphasises that our faith needs to be demonstrated by our deeds, our way of life. What are these deeds?

In chapter 1 James lists the following:

- Practical faith is humbly accepting, even welcoming, troubles. 'Consider it pure joy, my brothers and sisters, whenever you face trials of many kinds' (James 1:2). They work on our patient endurance. They build character in us.
- Practical faith is having the humility to ask God for wisdom, and the confidence that He will give it.
- Practical faith is seen when the socially humiliated

rejoice in their dignity in Christ, and the rich rejoice in the vulnerability of humility.
- Practical faith is worked out by resisting temptation, rather than succumbing to self-centred lust.
- Practical faith is being swift to hear, slow to anger and choosing words carefully (controlling the tongue).
- True religion is practical faith, caring for orphans and widows, and it is integrity, being unpolluted by the world.

In chapter 2 James expands on what it means to have an impartial attitude toward the poor and the rich.

> Has not God chosen those who are poor in the eyes of the world to be rich in faith and to inherit the kingdom he promised to those who love him? (James 2:5)

True humility does not try to impress the rich and influential. Practical faith is living a life of love.

> If you really keep the royal law found in Scripture, 'Love your neighbour as yourself,' you are doing right (James 2:8).

It is not good enough to just wish the needy well. Real faith is shown by showing practical care for the destitute.

> ...faith by itself, if it is not accompanied by action, is dead (James 2:17).

In chapter 3 James expands on the controlled use of the tongue. Practical faith is being reticent to judge and 'lecture' others. A judgmental attitude is an expression of pride, not humility. Pulling down others by our speech can destroy the whole of our Christian witness. Destructive criticism of others undermines all the good words we have otherwise spoken.

Speaking of two kinds of wisdom, James explains that a good life is lived by deeds done in humility, out of the wisdom of meekness, rather than the wisdom of the world, which is characterised by envy, selfish ambition and strife.

In chapter 4 James explains that contentious quarrels stem from selfish desires. Practical faith is not asking God for things to fulfil our own desires, but rather for the good of others. Who do we think we are if we think God is there to fulfil our will, our pleasure, rather than His? 'God opposes the proud but shows favour to the humble' (James 4:6). Practical faith is submitting to God and His will. It is resisting the devil's temptations to seek selfish pleasure. He then reiterates his warnings about prideful judgmentalism.

Then, at the end of chapter 4 and the beginning of chapter 5 James points out that practical faith is not being proud of our financial security. It is not living to make money or seeking pleasure. It is not exploiting workers, but rather it is being trusted to keep our promises.

Finally, he explains that practical faith is patiently waiting for the Lord to answer our prayer of faith and humbly restoring someone who has sinned. Practical faith is action enabling restoration.

It becomes clear that these deeds of faith are not specific

cultural forms of either the Jews or the Gentiles. They are not rules or rituals. They are dispositions and ways of relating to others, motivated by selfless love. They are equally applicable today as they were to the world of the New Testament.

The more I read the book of James, the more I see that the practice of the Christian life is based on the surety of our faith, and it is shown by humbly practising sacrificial love. Yes, the practice of humility is surely an integral part of our life in Christ!

So what does the practice of humility look like in our everyday context?

An anonymous person is not in a position to be any more prescriptive than James, who was writing to people in various places and circumstances. Indeed, making specific rules to be generally applied would be an act of arrogance, and it would be contrary to the spirit of the New Testament as explained in this book.

Someone closer to us, knowing our position and calling in life and our specific circumstances, and to whom we give permission to speak into our situation, may be free to be more explicit, as Paul was to some of those to whom he wrote.

Clearly, in each situation we need to be guided by the Word, the specific context, and the Holy Spirit as we decide what we do. With that in mind, I will offer the following imaginary scenarios as a sample of what humility might look like in different scenarios in the lives of Christians today.

I am an affluent American evangelical. I believe God has called me to bring the gospel to people in a slum in São Paulo, Brazil. I sell my house and move to Brazil and live in a house similar to the houses of those with whom I am called to share the good news of Jesus. In doing so, I am well aware I am putting myself in a vulnerable position. My health, my safety and my reputation are all at risk. But by sharing in the Brazilians' lives, learning their culture and adopting the cultural forms compatible with being a believer in Christ, I am able to model positive lifestyle choices and mentor them in their relationship with the Lord.

I am a local manager of a successful retail business. One of my junior managers makes a mistake in their processes. It has severe consequences for the business. I report it to my seniors as my error in not leading him well. I am risking my reputation and my position but demonstrating the love of Christ to others.

I have a Christian friend who has got caught up in an offbeat controversial doctrine. He is only listening to others who are also of this persuasion, the online echo-chamber feeding on this idea. He needs to listen to others whom I believe have a balanced understanding of the truth. He needs my love. He needs me to get under his skin, as it were, to understand and guide him. But spending significant time in conversation with him could be seen as being complicit in his heresy. I could become a victim of guilt by association. However, I am called to love others in Christ unconditionally, not just those who have their doctrine right from my perspective. Keeping in mind that he may become contentious and cast me away, I push ahead and make him a closer friend.

I am a follower of Christ in Delhi, India. I am a Brahmin, a member of the highest (priestly) social class. I am part of a local church which has members from different social classes. In various practical ways I assist a sick fellow believer who is a Dalit, a member of the social 'out caste'. I serve her Communion. In the opinion of many, including those in positions of authority, I am behaving disgracefully. I am incurring humiliation. I do not waver in my resolve to humbly serve others.

I am offered a promotion at my work. The managers discern I have a gift of decisiveness in my leadership. I defer my decision to accept the promotion until I have discussed it with my wife for her opinion and agreement.

I live next to a family whose way of life is 'questionable'. I don't want them to influence our children. I am given a substantial raise in my salary. In talking it through with my family, we decide to not 'improve' our own lifestyle, but rather share some of our income with the family next door as they are struggling to make ends meet and need to experience God's love for them.

I am a well-liked leader of the youth in my church. Unnoticed (to the best of my knowledge) by the youth, I also regularly clean the bathrooms.

I am hurt by my employer. He shows great disrespect towards me and is sometimes verbally abusive. On these occasions I remind myself who I am in Christ. I revisit my employer's business objectives and determine to do my best to serve him with these in mind. Nevertheless, I determine to speak to him about his approach. Appealing to his objectives, I ask him to understand how I feel when he speaks to me without respect. I leave it to him to respond with some change in his behaviour, and trust God to continue to do a good work in me for His glory.

I am a fellow-worker in the office of the disrespected employee. I am well-liked by our employer and in line for promotion. I risk my reputation with him by quietly speaking to him about what I have observed. I point out her faithful service to the company and her need for recognition or encouragement.

As a successful leader of a church I founded, I am faced with the people of the church wanting to express their appreciation of my inspirational leadership by giving me a very high salary and providing me with a luxurious house in which to live. What do I do? I decide to thank them for their love and appreciation and decline their offer, as it threatens the good reputation of the church and its ministry, and it distances me from the people whom I love and am called to serve.

As an adviser to churches I am invited to help a church

which has some leadership issues. The church leaders have been staunchly advocating that women should not be in any leadership positions. There are some women members who, from my conversation with them, seem to have leadership gifts and appropriate character qualities. I do not advise these women to insist they have a calling from God to lead and need recognition, but rather I tell them to serve the body humbly as the leaders require and to do it with wholehearted modesty and gracefulness. I advise the leaders to reconsider the truth of our equality and unity in Christ and to recognise the gifts and calling of God in the lives of all believers and how this should work out in the life of the church. Both these approaches put the ball in the court of those who are in a position to practice humility.

I am thanked for presenting a message of hope and encouragement at our small group meeting. I resist responding by saying it was nothing, but rather thank them for their appreciation and encourage them also to thank the Lord. At the end of the day I privately give God the glory.

I find myself in a rather public 'discussion' about a significant aspect of the Christian faith. I am aggressively asked a question about which I will be embarrassed if I do not confidently answer. I quietly say that I do not know how to answer that question, and that I will have to do some research to find the answer.

Each of us can identify with at least some of the above scenarios, and many more could have been described. Each of us has our own life calling in which to 'work out our salvation with fear and trembling'. We can humbly let the kingdom of God be worked out through our lives.

REFLECTIONS

In a discussion group, choose a difficult situation in which you may find yourself – maybe one from the list of scenarios in this chapter. Is there just one right way to act?

List some different ways of dealing with it. Discuss the pros and cons of the alternative choices of action.

Which alternatives are likely to be the most effective in bringing about a positive change?

What role do humility and sacrificial love play in the answer?

14

THE PRACTICE OF HUMILITY
IN WORKING OUT GOD'S GREAT PLAN

Elizabeth Gurney was a party girl. Her parents were wealthy bankers. Their religion was merely the expected formal attendance of Sunday worship. Their family home, Earlham Hall, was a centre for high society in Norwich, England. Being very articulate and never lacking admirers, Elizabeth enjoyed wearing brightly-coloured clothes and being the centre of the party. But, feeling unfulfilled, she sought God – unsuccessfully. After hearing the gospel preached by an American preacher, however, she realised the reality of God and Christ's death to save her.

Her purpose in life changed radically. No longer did she seek personal fulfilment in pleasure or religious duty; but accepting fulfilment in Christ, she now focused on loving God by loving others. She sought avenues to serve others. These included visiting the sick, making clothes for the poor, and starting a Sunday school for poor children to learn to read and write. To relate better to the people, she gave up the party life and the elaborate clothes that went with it.

She married Joseph Fry, a tea and spice merchant, and found herself focused on family life. But, about ten years later, with the approval of her husband, Elizabeth was once again initiating these sorts of endeavours in her community, now in Essex. She was also registered by the local Society of Friends as a minister, preaching around England about 'the grace of God to all'.

In 1813 she became aware of the shocking plight of prisoners in Newgate Prison. This led to her most noted service to the community – ministry to prisoners. Over the ensuing years, she initiated many projects to improve the life of the prisoners and their families. Stepping down from her life of privilege, she spent much of her days alongside these families whom society had rejected – reading the Bible and praying with them, feeding them, advocating for them and seeing many lives morally turned around. Her success brought invitations to initiate the same work in various parts of England and as far away as Russia. Government authorities took notice and legislation to improve the lot of prisoners and convict deportees followed.

The life of Elizabeth Fry is one of thousands of examples over the centuries of Christians who have responded to the grace of God in their lives by taking the humble path of sacrificially loving others.

When we peruse history, we see that this active kind of humility, where people deliberately chose to put themselves low for the sake of others, did not come to the fore until the 2nd to 5th century AD. It seems that it was a result of the influence of Christianity on the Roman world. Christians were seen to suffer martyrdom, willingly risking their own lives to save and care for others. They risked catching diseases and suffering violence by caring for the outcasts of Roman society. They practised what James encouraged, counting it joy to suffer for living for Jesus and others. The humility of the faithful changed the whole Roman Empire.

Sadly, as the church became more institutionalised and more removed from the simplicity of the good news of Jesus, many, even church leaders, were clearly not humble. It appears they often lost the vision of humble sacrificial love as taught in the New Testament. And there were pockets of the false humility of asceticism which has been previously mentioned. However, humility was a characteristic often seen in the monks who withdrew from the established church (and so were called 'secular'). Based in monasteries and in the community, they practised the humble Christian life of serving others.

Over the centuries there are many stories of men and women living lives of sacrificial love and humility. Among them were missionaries, community workers, health workers, servant leaders, practical servers and family leaders, all in their particular field, serving people as to the Lord. And most assuredly, there have been many, many more who have lived for Christ in this way, quietly doing the will of God, unnoticed by historians – unheralded 'Mother Theresas'. As Jesus said, they have their reward coming.

Having seen how the Biblical narrative has profoundly changed the shape of human civilisation through the lives of those who have themselves been reshaped by the gospel of

Christ, we are led to ask the question, 'What would the world be like without the good news of Jesus?' And specifically we could ask, 'What difference would there be in families, communities, nations and the whole world if people were not influenced to love sacrificially and show humility in their world?'

Would there have been men like 'Good King Wenceslas'? Vaclav the Good, the Duke of Bohemia, lived in the 10th century, when the lust for prestige and power led to assassinations and wars to overpower neighbouring domains. As the Christmas carol describes, he went out at night to give alms to widows, orphans, the sick and prisoners. His younger brother, who despised his attitude of humility, waged war against him. He chose to risk his own life rather than see his subjects suffer death in war, and so was brutally killed by his brother's men. Because of his piety and 'martyrdom', he was subsequently declared 'King' and 'Saint' Wenceslas.

Would there have been any nations where kings surrendered their power to the common people and allowed the political systems of 'democracy' to develop incrementally? Would nations ever have begun to talk with each other and seek to understand others' perspectives rather than just want to dominate their neighbours?

Without the rediscovery of the message of the New Testament, would 'Christendom' still lord it over others? Would the Western world still justify systems of racial discrimination such as slavery, if men like William Wilberforce had not pursued their calling? Appealing to Christian values, he sought to persuade the nation to love all humans humbly, regardless of their race and to outlaw the slave trade and slavery itself. Without Christ, would there have been humble Christian men and women like Martin Luther King Jr making themselves vulnerable to humiliation and even death for the sake of others?

Without the development of the Christian understanding of the equal value of men and women, would most men still dominate over women and regard them as resources to achieve their purposes? Without the Christian conscience in the Western world, would rich leaders of industry still exploit their workers and have no concern for their welfare, health and safety? Would there have been humble men of God such as George Cadbury setting an example for others to follow?

Without Christ, our world would unquestionably be dominated by the self-seeking, those who lust after prestige and power. But because of many humble servants of Jesus, this is not universally so. Authoritarian leaders do not have all the say and do not have all the sway.

The kingdom of God is still very much a work in progress. Sometimes we are tempted to despair when we see the fruit of power-seeking, corruption and outright pride being worked out in our communities and nations. There is still a very long way to go.

But God has got it. He is working out His plan. And it won't be worked out by us seeking power and control, albeit to do good, but rather by the persuasive power of the humility of Christ in us. One life at a time, following Christ, working humbly in community, changing the world!

REFLECTIONS

Discuss how your future may be different as a result of engaging with the ideas and issues raised in this book.

How will you practise life differently?

APPENDIX 1

CONTRASTING LIFE IN THE NATURAL WITH LIFE IN THE SPIRITUAL

Regarding:	The Natural Life (in Adam)	The Spiritual Life (in Christ)
Sin and righteousness (see Romans 8)	We are all sinners We choose to sin We deserve death	We are redeemed We choose to accept His forgiveness, His grace We receive life
Our status, dignity and prestige (see Ephesians 1-3)	It's a matter of honour and shame It's a matter of achieving dignity	It is knowing God accepts us and speaks well of us It is accepting dignity in Christ
Our motivation (see 1 Corinthians 13)	Self-centredness Self-promotion	Other-centredness Love
Our dispositions	Independence Assertiveness Contentiousness Divisiveness Pride	Interdependence Deferring to the other Peacemaking Unity Humility
Men and women (see 1 Corinthians 11, Ephesians 5)	Man was made first Women were made for men Men lead, women obey	We are all recreated one in Christ together We submit to one another

Appendix 1

Rights	Claiming or asserting our own rights	Respecting and working for the rights of others
Leadership	Dominating Controlling	Inspiring Serving in love Setting an example
People in authority (see e.g. Romans 13)	We are obliged to submit to the law	We honour and therefore obey authorities

APPENDIX 2

LIVING IN THE LIGHT OF GRACE: LICENCE, LEGALISM OR LIBERTY?

	Life without the revelation of God	Life with the revelation of the Law	Life with the revelation of the New Testament
Based on:	Not recognising or thanking God	Righteousness by keeping the Law	Righteousness achieved by Christ and received by faith
Motivated by:	Personal ambition, desire	Obligation	Loving God and others, the good of others
Centre of worship:	Idolatory – living for personal (selfish) goals, God-hating (theophobia)	God Fearing God	God Fearing and loving God
Guided by:	Lust, licentiousness	Rules, regulations	The Holy Spirit
Constrained by:	Social pressure	Fear of failure	The love of God

Appendix 2

Characterised by:	Envy, strife, arrogance, deceit, malice, slander, etc. (see e.g. Romans 1, Galatians 5:19-21)	The bondage of attempting to keep the Law, e.g. Ten Commandments, circumcision, tithing, food laws, ceremonial calendar, etc. (600+ laws)	Sacrificial love, humility, e.g. love, joy, peace, longsuffering, kindness, goodness, faithfulness, meekness, self-control (Galatians 5:22-23)
Ultimate destiny:	I did it my way – death	I failed to do it – death	Jesus did it in me – eternal life

As the Epistles repeatedly point out, we who have faith in Christ are urged to live the life of love in the Spirit of Christ, (e.g. Galatians 5), not reverting to the bondage of the Old Testament law nor to a new set of 'Christian' laws (e.g. dress codes, tithing by obligation, eating the right foods, legalistic Sabbath-keeping), nor reverting to the way of life of the 'world' with its self-centred ambitions, lusts, materialism and the like (e.g. 1 John 2:15-17).

BACKGROUND READING

Scripture references are cited on the page where they are quoted.

After embarking on writing this book, a friend recommended that I should read John Dickson's book:

Dickson J. *Humilitas: A lost key to life, love and leadership*. Grand Rapids, Mich.: Zondervan, 2011.

I commend it to anyone who wants to better understand humility. It examines humility from an historian's perspective. The author says, 'My thesis is simple: The most influential and inspiring people are often marked by humility.' One significant observation he makes is along these lines: When you examine the history of the notion and practice of humility, Jesus is clearly the game-changer.

ALSO BY JOHN NORSWORTHY

Why Culture Matters: A biblical Christian approach to things cultural. Tauranga, New Zealand: ConsultEd Publishing, 2009.

Why Science Matters: What does the Bible say about things scientific? Tauranga, New Zealand: ConsultEd Publishing, 2018.

Educating Our Children Faithfully: The story of the NZ Christian school movement 1964-2014. New Zealand Association for Christian Schools, 2014.

www.ingramcontent.com/pod-product-compliance
Lightning Source LLC
Chambersburg PA
CBHW051405290426
44108CB00015B/2157